KG55

Greif

Geschwader

Steve Hall
and
Lionel Quinlan

**RED
KITE**

First published 2000 by
Red Kite
PO Box 223,
Walton on Thames
Surrey, KT12 3YQ

© 2000 Steve Hall and Lionel Quinlan

Printed in Malta by
Interprint.

ISBN 0-9538061-0-3

Contents

Introduction

The history of Kampfgeschwader 55 "Greif" can be traced back to April 1934 and was among the first units of the Luftwaffe to receive Ernst Heinkel's advanced bomber, the He111. Remarkably for any Luftwaffe unit, KG55 kept the Heinkel as its principal machine for the entire war. Even in the dying days of Hitler's Reich the latest variants of the He111 were in action on the Russian Front.

Our aim in producing this book was to provide, as broadly as possible, a photographic record of the men and machines of Kampfgeschwader 55 "Greif" Many of the crew members were to see their first action serving with the "Condor Legion" during the Spanish Civil War, in support of General Franco's Fascist forces. During the month of September 1939 the unit was involved in the attack on Poland. When Poland's capital, Warsaw, capitulated on 27 September, 1939, KG 55 was moved back to air-fields in Germany in preparation for the attack on France. They were to be involved in this campaign from October 1939 until 25 June, 1940, when France too capitulated. When operations in the Battle of Britain began, casualties began to mount alarmingly, but the tempo was maintained throughout the Blitz. In July 1941, KG55 began its operations on the Russian Front, where the majority of the unit fought through the next four years of horror and slaughter.

The collection of material relating to KG55 is an on-going project, which is far from complete. We therefore welcome your comments and additions that should be sent to us via the publisher.

Lionel Quinlan and Steve Hall

Acknowledgements

We have been very fortunate to receive help and encouragement from many of the ex-members of Kamfgeschwader 55 and their relatives, as well as people from this side of The Channel. Had it not been for them providing photographs, information, and their memories this project would have been impossible.

Most of the photographs are from private collections, whilst others are from sources which are not known. As a result those photographs which appear where clearance has not been given, is unintentional.

Those who did help we ask to accept our sincere thanks for their time and trouble. They are:- Kurt Baumann, Heinrich Becker, Anton Bell, Heiner Blanz, Fritz Bohmichen, Kurt Böker, Josef Boos, Ludwig Brossler, Karl Brüning, Richard Brunner, Patrick Burgess, Magdalene Burmeier, Egon Buschgen, Ron Collier, Guy Coquillat, R.W. Cox, A.G. Croad, Walter Dietrich, Georg Engel (+ 4.2.1994), Kurt Gerhard Franke, Wolfgang Glieden, Rheinhard Haase, Elfriede Hahn, Max Hausdörfer, Heinrich Hennecke, Friedrich Jordan, Martin Junglehner, Wilhelm Kempel, Reimer Kruse, Thea Link, Marga Lösch, Josef Luxenburger, Waltraut Müller-Mamerow, Lizzi Meier, Charlotte Michel. Jens Möhn, Hans Mössner, Hans Moritz, Adam Muhn, Godfrey Nall, Herta Nordhaub, Fritz Pons (+ 6.7.1994), Johann Raths, Margarete Reis, Derek Round, Heinz Sabiel, Andy Saunders, Dietrich Schaefer, Karl Scheuringerg Walter Schmid, Siegfried Schweinhagen, Konrad Soieshofer, Alois Stadel, Wilhelm Steinmann, Peggy and Chris Stephenson, Hans Strobel, Elli Sturat, Hans Thurnheer, Hans Unmack, Willy Vrolike, Kenneth Wakefield, Willi Wazek, Franz Weinert, Peter White and Max Wiederer.

We would also wish to acknowledge the invaluable help given to us by innumerable Bürgermeisters, Deutsche Dienststelle (Wast) and Volksbund Deutsche Kriegsgräberfürsorge e.V.

Finally we wish to place on record our sincere thanks to Simon Parry for all his help, hard work and encouragement.

Early Days

1936 - Hans Unmack takes his first steps towards becoming a pilot in KG55.

KG55 can trace its origin back to 1934 when, on 1 April, a unit known as Hanseatische Fliegerschule e. V. was formed. It was based at Fassberg where it shared the airfield with 1., 2., and 3. Staffeln of KG154. On 24 October 1938 Stab KG155, as it had by now been redesignated, was based at Giessen with II./KG155. I./KG155 was based at Langendiebach.

The designation Kampfgeschwader 55 'Greif' was adopted on 1 May 1939, with Stab, I., and II., Gruppen. III., Gruppe was not created until December 1939.

Pre-war equipment included the He111 *Langnaseu.*

Richard Bock was typical of many early pilots who trained on gliders and went on to become operational pilots. Seen here in pre-war days, he flew with KG55 in Europe and Russia before he was shot down over England on 30 July 1942.

Generalmajor Wilhelm Süssmann was KG55's first Geschwaderkommodore, from March 1937 to 6 March 1940. He was awarded the Ritterkreuz on 9 July 1941, but was killed later that year when Kommodore of 7 Fliegerdivision in Crete. (Jens Möhn)

John-Christian Möhn (left) examines the damage to his He111 G1+BA after it was hit by AA fire over Poland on 7 September 1939. The officer on the right is Walter Kleinhanns, who was killed over Britain on 12 July 1940 when acting as observer to Möhn.
Note the unusual style of the fuselage markings. (Jens Möhn)

He111P, G1+FA of Geschwaderstab KG55 runs up its engines at Breslau during the Polish campaign. (Hans Strobl)

On 12 September 1939 Herman Goring visited the Stab of KG55 at Marzdorf/Ohlau. The officer in the white dress cap is Generalmajor Süssmann. (Hans Strobl)

During the Polish campaign, KG55 lost only one Heinkel and crew. Oberleutnant Walter Fritz and his 1/KG55 crew were killed in a crash near Chyrov, south-west of L'vov, Poland. The Geschwaderstab had an aircraft damaged by Polish fighters on 11 September 1939 and Oberleutnant Heinz Hofer was forced to land between the lines. The crew were rescued by German troops and returned in a Ju52 the next day. Other casualties of the campaign were Uffz Karl Rathmann of the Geschwaderstab, who was wounded on 13 September, and another He111 was damaged in a forced landing near Warsaw on 14 September.

Battle of France

Leutnant Hans Junk (left) was hit in the head and died instantly when G1+DM was attacked on 12 May, 1940. Unteroffiziers Thone and Ege, with Gerfreiter Wendt were killed, only the observer Unteroffizier Rasper survived. (Charlotte Michel)

Following the Polish campaign, KG55 moved to various bases in Germany in preparation for the invasion of France. The crews had suffered few losses over Poland, but the French and RAF fighters proved to be more formidable opponents and casualties soon began to increase.

On 10 May, 1940, the Stab./KG55 began operations in the area of Nancy - Toul - Epinal. Twelve fighters attacked and wounded three crewmen on board one of the Heinkels. The targets for 12 May were railway lines near Rethel, to the north east of Reims. Fighters brought down G1+DM of 4./KG55, the first casualty of the Battle of France.

Six aircraft were lost on 13 May. G1+GA of Stab./KG55 went down near Vouziers, G1+FN of 5./KG55 made it to German held territory in Belgium, and three machines from 6./KG55 and one from 8./KG55 were lost attacking troops in the Charleville - Mezieres area. Another two Heinkels returned to base severely damaged and with wounded crew on board. In just three days KG55 had suffered more casualties than in the whole of the Polish campaign.

Oberleutnant Clem von Hohenberg's G1+GA was hit by AA fire over Vouziers on 13 May and he was forced to crash land by fighters. Obergefreiter Hans Bell (left) suffered a severe injury to his upper right thigh and was carried to a nearby wood by the rest of the crew including Feldwebel Willi Wolter (right). As French troops approached, Hohenberg gave the order to flee towards the German lines. Wolter went to Bell to tell him of the plan, but was shot several times in the stomach and was dead on arrival at the French hospital set up a school in Vouziers. Hans Bell passed away in the same hosptial later that day. Hohenberg, Unteroffizier Strobl, and Gerfeiter Männer were taken prisoner. (Anton Bell)

Oberleutnant Weigel was on his third sortie of the day on 13 May when his He111P was attacked and shot down by five Morane Saulnier MS406 fighters. The attack damaged the port engine, but Weigel crossed the German lines and crash landed safely near Attert, Belgium. (Georg Engel)

This crew of 8./KG55 was shot down in G1+HS on 13 May, 1940. It was crash landed near Vendresse, France, and was destroyed by the crew before they made their escape to the German lines. Left to right they were: Oberfeldwebel Hickel (pilot), Gefreiter Bodenhagen (gunner), Feldwebel Herzog (engineer), Hausdörfer (observer), and Gerfeiter Arndt (wireless operator).

On 2 June, 1940, KG55 attempted to bomb Lyon/Bron airfield, but strayed into Swiss airspace and were intercepted by Bf109E-3s of 15 Fliegerkompanie Swiss airforce. Capitaine Hans Thurnheer (left) shot down G1+HS, an He111P-2 of 8./KG55 flown by Unteroffizier Horst Mahnert. The aircraft (below) landed near Ursins at the southern end of Lac de Neuchatel. Gefreiter Lindner died of wounds, but the other four men were interned. (Thurnheer)

Unteroffizier Kurt Schraps and his crew walked away from this He111 P-2 after crash landing due to failure of the port engine on return from a raid to Paris in June 1940.

The nose mounted 7.92mm MG 15 and bomb sight below the nose. The panel in the top of the cockpit has been left open.

The propeller and reduction gear of the DB601A engine has been ripped away.

During the French campaign, KG55 lost thirty-four aircraft with thirty-nine aircrew killed, ninety-three wounded and nine men missing.

Battle of Britain

The locals look on as Oberleutnant Schweinhagen's Heinkel burns on East Beach, Selsey, Sussex. G1+LK of 2./KG55 was shot down by Hurricane pilots of No. 145 Squadron on 11 July, 1940, while attacking Portsmouth.

KG55 Organisation for the Battle of Britain.

Stab KG55   Base: Villacoublay 21 June 1940 to 16 June 1941.
              Aircraft on strength: 9 (6 servicable) at 17 August 1940.
              Commanding Officers: Oberst Stoeckl to 14 August 1940;
              Oberstleutnant Korte to 31 January 1941.
I./KG55   Base: Villacoublay 23 June 1940 to 1 August 1940; Dreux until
              14 April 1941; Melun/Villaroche until 12 June 1941.
              Aircraft on strength: 32 (27 servicable) at 17 August 1940.
              Commanding Officer: Major Roeber to 13 February 1941.
II./KG55   Base: Villacoublay 23 June 1940 to 1 August 1940; Chartres
              until 18 June 1941.
              Aircraft on strength: 32 (26 servicable) at 17 August 1940.
              Commanding Officers: Oberstleutnant Lachemair to 27 July 1940;
              Major Kless to 27 October 1940; Major Gabriel to 31 March 1941.
III./KG55   Base: Villacoublay 23 June 1940 to 18 June 1941.
              Aircraft on strength: 34 (23 servicable) at 17 August 1940.
              Commanding Officers: Major Schemmell to 30 September 1940;
              Hauptman Wittmer to 1 September 1941.

The Glorious Twelfth. Six Hurricane pilots of No. 43 Squadron 'bagged' **G1+FA** of the Geschwader Stab KG55 during an attack on Portsmouth on 12 July 1940. Oberleutnant Kleinhanns was killed, but the other four crew were captured after the Heinkel landed near the 'Horse and Jockey', Hipley, near Portsmouth.

Feldwebel John-Christian Möhn was the pilot of G1+FA when it was shot down.

Scars left by No. 43 Squadron's guns. The tail of G1+FA showing some of the damage to the control surfaces.

The damaged dorsal gun position is visible here against the trees.

Feldwebel Theodore Metzner, pilot of G1+CS which crashed near Newbury. Metzner was one of the first to be taken prisoner. (Pons)

Feldwebel Josef Markl, holds the distinction of staying on the run longer than any other downed Luftwaffe airman in Britain. On 29 July, 1940, he was the observer aboard G1+CS during an attack on Bristol. Anti aircraft fire damaged the controls, port wing and engine, forcing the crew to bale out before the Heinkel crashed in Fullers Lane, near Newbury. Metzner and Unteroffizier Böker were first to be captured, Gefreiters Ostheimer and Morgenthal stayed at large for 48 hours, but of Josef Markl there was not a trace. He landed in trees and, after extracting himself, destroying his papers and hiding his flying gear, he set out to give himself up in Newbury. After wandering around the town Markl considered he would rather be captured than surrender himself, so he settled down in an area of nettles and bracken some 500 yards out of town. Here he stayed, eating crops from the fields and drinking a little water. He even made some forays around his neighbourhood, but eventually, on Bank Holiday Monday, 5 August, he decided to give himself up. Weak from hunger, Markl walked in the rain to Newbury where a man and girl on bicycles saw him - and rode away at speed. One car passed him by, but a second stopped and reversed back along the road to him. In the car was Lady Buckland, who instructed her chauffeur, Mr Nicholls, to drive to the police station. Josef Markl surrendered his pistol and 16 rounds of ammunition before being taken into custody for the duration. He later remarked he had been, 'Agreeably surprised' at the way he had been treated.

The burnt out wreckage of G1+CS at Fullers Lane, Newbury, Berkshire. (Newbury Weekly News)

Feldwebel Josef Markl

Unteroffizier Kurt Böker

Gefreiter Ernst Ostheimer

Oberfeldwebel Gerhard Geissler was the pilot of G1+IR from 7./KG55 which was lost during a mission to attack Manchester on the night of 4 August. Only Geissler's body was found, washed up on a beach near Le Havre, no trace of the four other men was found. (Herta Nordhaub)

Oberst Alois Stoeckl

Oberleutnant Bruno Brossler

KG55 lost its Geschwaderkommodore on 14 August, when He111P, G1+AA, was shot down by Spitfire pilots of No. 609 Squadron. The Heinkel fell at the Royal Naval Armament Depot, Dean Hill, Romsey, Hampshire. Three of the crew were killed including Stoeckl and Brossler.

He111P, G1+LM of 4./KG55 exploded after crashing at Upper Frithfold Farm, Northchapel, Sussex, on 16 August. The explosion damaged the Hurricane of Pilot Officer Goodman, who was circling 500 feet above his victim. All five men were killed including Hauptman Wladimir Sabler, Staffelkapitän of 4./KG55 since April 1939.

6./KG55 lost G1+HP on 16 August 1940 during the attack on Feltham, near London. Gunfire from Squadron Leader Pemberton's No. 1 Squadron Hurricane damaged the oil cooling system causing failure of the engines. The pilot, Oberleutnant Wilhelm Wieland, brought the Heinkel down to a good landing at Annington Farm, Bramber, Sussex.

Unteroffizier Gerhard Pulver who, with Unteroffizier Anton Hattendorf, died of wounds in G1+HP.

Gordon James took this photo at Oakhill, Bursledon, Hampshire, as the remains of G1+HP were transported to a scrap yard. It was against the law to take such photos, so Mr James kept his camera hidden until after the war, when he finally had the film developed. (Peter White)

G1+FR of 7./KG55 was also shot down on the 16 August raid to Feltham, west of London. Flight Lieutenant Boyd of No. 602 Squadron put between 300 and 400 bullet holes in the bomber before it crashed at Honeysuckle Lane, High Salvington, Sussex. Of the crew, pilot Leutnant Rudolf Theopold, observer Unteroffizier Rudolf Hornbostel and wireless operator Gefreiter Helmut Glaser, were taken prisoner. Flight engineer Unteroffizier Albert Weber and gunner Gefreiter Johannes Moorfeld were both killed.

"During the late afternoon of 16 August, 1940, I (a soldier on leave) was going for a walk over the Downs. As I came to the end of Honeysuckle Lane, where it adjoins a small sloping field, I heard a great noise of a very low-flying 'plane midst much machine-gun fire. Suddenly, as I flung myself into a hedge, I saw a Heinkel 111 bomber fly just over my head and land very heavily in the field ahead. There were no other people about as I rushed to the 'plane to help the crew get out. After a few minutes some British soldiers from an observation post further up the hill appeared and took the crew, and me, prisoner. I had spent the previous year with a German speaking family in Poland so I was able to talk to the crew in German. I was wearing civilian cloths, and I was unable to convince the soldiers that I was not part of the crew. They locked me in the ambulance with the German airmen, two dead, two wounded and one unhurt. They took us to Worthing hospital and then took me to the Police station where I was interrogated before being finally driven home.

"Throughout the ordeal I was very impressed by the calmness of the officer, whom I presumed to be the pilot. He asked me where they were, then could I give him a cigarette and, finally, would I retrieve his cap which he had left in the cockpit. He thought it unlikely that he would be able to obtain a replacement for a while! However, he complained bitterly at the very un-British way that the fighters continued pumping bullets into the 'plane, killing two of his men, just as his 'plane was crashing.

"Some days later I was allowed to visit the two wounded Germans, in Worthing hospital, and took them some cigarettes and sweets, much to the disgust of the other patients in the ward."

Derek A. Round.

Some of the damage caused by
Boyd's bullets.

An innocent victim of war!
The soldiers are carrying 7.92mm
ammunition drums from MG15s

Feldwebel Hans Reiter (observer) and Oberleutnant Hans Mössner pilot (right) crash landed their Heinkel G1+EK near Le Havre after it was damaged by fighters on 23 August, 1940.

Oberfeldwebel Otto Weis, engineer (left) Oberfeldwebel Kurt Heinze, wireless operator (right) were also aboard G1+EK when it crashed. The fifth man was Gefreiter Harald Kawlath, who baled out over the Channel, never to be found.

G1+EK photographed in July 1940 at Villacoublay.

KG55 lost four Heinkels on 26 August 1940, during the attack on Portsmouth. G1+DM Wn. 2124 was shot down by Spitfire pilots of No. 602 Squadron and crashed on the beach at Bracklesham, Sussex.

Although seemingly little damaged only the pilot, Leutnant Albert Metzger, escaped with his life. Up to 500 bullet strikes were found in the wreck, many fired by troops as the Heinkel attempted to land.

The four fatalities were buried in Chichester Cemetery, but were later reinterred at Cannock Chase, Staffordshire.

Oberleutnant Ignaz Krenn was the pilot of G1+BB which he crash landed at Wick, Sussex, on 26 August, 1940. He was photographed at Chichester Station on his way to six years in captivity.

G1+BB where Iganz Krenn landed it at Wick.

The remains of G1+BB are carried away on two lorries.

"I looked at the land below to find a landing place, but then a village appeared with a row of trees behind it. With all my strength I pulled back on the stick and skimmed over the top. I cut the ignition and the 'plane careered over a grassy field, throwing up earth and stones with a terrible noise before finally coming to a rest near a stream. It had been the softest belly landing I could have wished for. My flight engineer tapped me on the shoulder and said, 'All change Oberleutnant, this is the end of the line.' We helped each other clamber out and stood on the grass, wiping sweat from our brows, we said nothing. Then a military vehicle drew up and what I took to be Home Guard got out. An elderly man in civilian clothes came up to me and asked in excellent German in anyone had been injured."

Ignaz Krenn.

The man who approached Krenn was Alfred Bowerman, owner of Court Wick Park Farm, where the Heinkel had landed. He recalled, "I only knew about five words of German, but was relieved that the pilot could speak English. He said, 'I suppose this is my Waterloo?' I then asked him to collect all their revolvers and jack-knives and hand them to me, which they did immediately. I assured him they had nothing to fear if they obeyed my orders, which they seemed most anxious to do. The pilot was very well spoken, courteous and obviously a very efficient Luftwaffe airman."

Another of the 26 August victims, G1+GM flown by Leutnant Klaus Walter of 4./KG55. Gunfire from a Hurricane flown by Pilot Officer North of No. 43 Squadron damaged the oil and coolant systems in the starboard engine which over heated and seized. The He111 hit a tree and broke in half at Westbrook Farm, Waterlooville, Hampshire.

The observer, Oberfeldwebel Otto Hennecke, baled out of G1+GM when it was too low and was killed, but the rest of the crew survived the rough landing. This photograph was taken after he received the Iron Cross Second Class on 10 November 1939. Otto Hennecke remains buried at Annes Hill Cemetery, Gosport, Hampshire.
(Heinrich Hennecke)

KG55 Losses on 26 August, 1940. Target Portsmouth.

G1+BB   He111P Stab I./ KG55 Wick, Sussex.
G1+DM   He111P 4./KG55 Bracklesham, Sussex.
G1+GM   He111P 4./KG55 Waterlooville, Hampshire.
G1+GN   He111P 5./KG55 English Channel off Sussex.

Rescued from the sea, the crew of G1+GN.

Brüning checks on his wounded flight engi
neer, Unteroffizier Lösch. (Marga Lösch)

Feldwebel Karl Brüning was the pilot of G1+GN when it was shot
down by Pilot Officer Aries flying a Spitfire of No. 602 Squadron
on the 26 August raid. The crew was picked up by the
Seenotdienst. Three of the crew, including Unteroffizier Willi
Lösch (left) were injured.

Safely aboard the Seenotdienst
launch. Karl Brüning (far right)
and Oberleutnant Fritz von dem
Hagen (left foreground).
(Brüning)

Arno Raths was buried with his fellow crew members at Versailles, near Paris.

Obergefreiter Arno Raths, gunner aboard G1+KS when it crashed. (Johann Raths)

August 30, 1940, was a day of great activity over Britain, yet KG55 lost no aircraft in combat. Unusually though, four Heinkels crashed that day in France. Two crews from II. Gruppe collided during a training flight near Chartres and all eight crew men were killed. G1+ES was damaged by anti-aircraft fire during an attack on Liverpool and crash landed near Sens, all five aboard were injured. Unteroffizier Müller was flying G1+KS near Versailles when he collided with another Heinkel from the Ergänzungsstaffel KG55 which was able to make a safe landing. Müller was unable to control his Heinkel and again all five were killed in the crash.

Two more Heinkels crashed in France on 7 September, 1940. One aircraft from Stab III./KG55 crashed near Dreux returning from London. The second machine, G1+DS of 8./KG55, (pictured right) crashed near Beauvais after the crew baled out following engine failure on return from London. (Hickel)

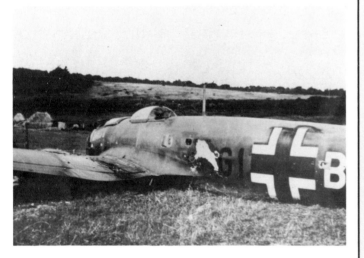

One of the four KG55 losses on the 25 September raid to Filton was G1+BH of 1./KG55. Feldwebel Fritz Jürges was obliged to make a forced landing at Westland Farm, near Swanage, Dorset, after repeated attacks from pilots of Nos. 609 and 238 Squadrons.

"At that time I was fourteen years of age living with my parents in the village of Studland. On that particular day I was with my father in the grounds of Studland Bay House, near the Knoll House Hotel. It was about mid-day and an air raid warning had been sounded. Other aircraft were, or had just been, overhead at some considerable altitude.

"I first saw this aircraft coming from the general direction of Sandbanks. It was at a height of but a few hundred feet barely maintaining airspeed with one engine out of action and the other not on full power. When almost overhead, with its markings clearly visible, it changed course to port, towards the fields on the cliff top near the Old Harry Rocks. At this time it was being pursued by four and possibly a fifth Spitfire. As the Heinkel began to carry out this manoeuvre one of the Spitfires fired a short burst of machine gun fire at it. I could hear the bullets striking the aircraft which then turned inland towards the west. It came down in a shallow dive with its wheels retracted, landing in a field on Westfield Farm which is situated along the Swanage road near the turning to Corfe Castle. As the Heinkel came down its starboard wing tip struck a wooden electricity standard in a field close to the farm house and the wing tip broke away. I did not see or hear any return fire from the Heinkel and at least one of the Spitfire aircraft performed a victory roll over the downed Heinkel before making off towards the coast.

"At the scene I saw two of the crew of the German aircraft in custody sitting in a car on the road just beyond the point where the road forks to the right towards Rempstone and Corfe Castle. One of them was forced to 'spend a penny' between the car and the hedge and it came as quite a shock to me at that age to realise that these were also human beings and not something from outer space.

"There was a further tragic incident when the downed aircraft was moved, as a jib of the crane used in the lifting operation came in contact with an overhead electric power cable. Three men were electrocuted and another was badly burned about the hands."

Mr. Peter Burchall

G1+DN (above) was another victim of 25 September's raid on the Bristol aero engine works at Filton. Oberleutnant Gottfreid Weigel and his crew baled out safely before the Heinkel crashed at Racecourse Farm, Portbury, near Bristol. An anti-aircraft shell fired by the 237th Battery, 76th HAA regiment based at Portbury had exploded under the Heinkel's tail and damaged its controls.

The wreckage of G1+DN was scattered over several hundred yards, but the bomb load did not explode.

Hauptman Hellmuth Brandt was the only one to escape from this wreck of G1+EP before it crashed at Church Farm, near Frome, Somerset. Again, this was a victim of the 25 September Bristol raid.

G1+LR photographed by Unteroffizier Kurt Schraps in formation.

The Heinkel was set upon by at least three fighters near Poole, Dorset, on 25 September, 1940, during the Bristol raid.

Unteroffizier Kurt Schraps floats down into Poole Harbour. He was the only man to survive as three others who baled out were found dead. Oberleutnant Scholz was found dead on the railway line near Sandbanks Road bridge. Unteroffizier Weidner's parachute failed and he fell onto a road. Unteroffizier Hanft landed in Poole harbour and was dead when recovered from the water.

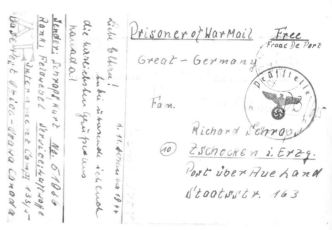

Schraps sent this post card from his Canadian prisoner of war camp in March, 1945. He did not return to Germany until 1947.

The attacking pilots were: Pilot Officers Agazarian and Miller in Spitfires of No. 609 Squadron and Pilot Officer Erwin-Mann in a No. 238 Squadron Hurricane.

Smoke rises from the site where G1+LR crashed on a house called Underwood, in Pinewood Road, Branksome, near Bournemouth.

Wireless operator Kurt Schraps, the sole survivor.

Unteroffizier Gunter Weidner, the flight engineer, was found dead after his parachute failed to open.

Unteroffizier Ernst Herber.

Leutnant Ulrich Flügge.

Feldwebel Ernst Ens.

Gefreiter Hans Pawlik.

The RAF airfield at Thorney Island was the target for 8./KG55 on 8 October, 1940.

Oberfeldwebel Fritz Pons was aboard G1+LS and has cause to remember the day well.

"My C.O. Oberleutnant Jürgen Bartens said to me that as it was my birthday we would go on a raid to England to celebrate. Three aircraft were detailed for the mission (Gl+LS, Gl+MS and G1+BS). The gunner of Gl+MS, Gefreiter Pawlik, was a special friend of mine. I was like a father to Pawlik, who was a happy and cheerful type, who before the war had been a barrow-boy selling fruit and vegetables in a German village. On this day I remember that Pawlik was very gloomy and told me that he would rather not go on the mission. Right up until the time of take off he remained with me and I tried to reassure him.

"Just before dusk the three machines took off from Villacoublay and set course for England, flying very low to escape detection by radar. On crossing the English coast we were surprised to see a Wellington taking off from an airfield directly ahead, it flew towards us and passed about 50 metres above. I recall plainly that there was nobody in the rear turret! The pilot of the Wellington had not seen our three He 111s. I asked my C.O. if I could open fire, but was told that it was not our duty on this mission and that we had something else to do. So we went on to bomb England and the British plane went out to bomb Germany.

"We flew low over a town and looked down a long straight road seeing the surprised faces of people looking up at us. A short time afterwards we were fired on by some light A.A. guns hidden in some trees on our left-hand side. I opened fire immediately with my twin MG 15 machine guns.

"As soon as I opened fire the ground fire ceased. I was however, aware of an explosion on my right-hand side. There was a huge mushroom cloud of smoke and fire coming from the trees below and there was only one aircraft following. My pilot, Oberfeldwebel Franz Vonier, shouted over the radio to me asking what had happened. I replied that it must have been Ens. There could have been no survivors.

"After the crash of Ens we went on to drop our bombs and then return home. This was Unteroffizier Meier, our gunner's, first low-level raid and he was rather excited. As a result he began machine gunning the airfield which alerted the defences and caused the Bofors A.A. guns to open fire. I realised that this fire would bring ground fire onto us and tried to stop Meier without success. I eventually threw my steel helmet at Meier, which had the desired effect. If I had been taken prisoner, my captors would have had a surprise as I was only wearing my flying suit with nothing underneath, as I had been working all day on the guns!

Fritz Pons.

Part of G1+MS under guard at Stansted Park, Stoughton, Sussex.

Fritz Pons' unusual twin machine gun mounting designed by him.

G1+BS was damaged and returned to Villacoublay with two wounded crew on board. The body of Feldwebel Ens was the only one of the four crew aboard G1+MS that could be identified and he was buried at St. Nicholas Churchyard, West Thorney. The diary for RAF Thorney Island records that one Douglas DB-7 was destroyed and one Blenheim damaged in the attack.

Major Dr. Ernst Kühl, seen above showing Generalfeldmarschall Kesselring the map, was aboard G1+JA of the Geschwaderstab KG55 when it was forced to land in the Channel off Cherbourg on 30 September. It is believed that the aircraft had been brought down by Pilot Officer Agazarian flying a Spitfire of No. 609 Squadron. Kühl had been acting as the observer and was rescued with injuries, only the pilot, Unteroffizier Barabas, was killed. KG55 was taking part in an attack on the Westland aircraft factory near Yeovil, Somerset that day and lost four Heinkels in the sea.

KG55 Losses 1 July 1940 to 30 October 1940

	100%	70-80%	45-60%	25-40%	20-25%
Stab.	6	1	0	1	0
I./KG55	10	2	2	5	2
II./KG55	11	0	3	3	5
III./KG55	16	2	2	6	1
Erg.St.	2	0	0	1	0
Total	45	5	7	16	8

G1+HS of 8./KG55 returned to Villacoublay on 20 October, 1940, but a 'hung-up' incendiary bomb ignited and set fire to the aircraft. Oberfeldwebel Bernhard Hickel and his crew escaped injury. (Hickel)

Major Friedrich Kless Gruppenkommandeur of II./KG55 was awarded the Ritterkreuz on 14 October, 1940.   (Kless)

He111 P-2 Wn. 2666 of Stab. KG55 (below) crashed at Villacoublay on return from a sortie to London on 26 October 1940. The damage was such that the aircraft was written off, but no casualties were reported. Note how the markings have been blacked out. (Hickel)

Night Blitz

Leutnant Hans-Adalbert Tüffers at the controls of an He111. On 1 November, 1940, during an attack on the Royal Victoria Docks, G1+JS was hit by anti aircraft fire and crashed at Matlock Gardens, Hornchurch, Essex. The Heinkel crashed in a street where burning wreckage set fire to the surrounding area. A commendation (below) was issued to three members of the Home Guard. (Ken Wakefield)

Warm commendation was given by the Zone Commander to Sgt. C.E. Strange, Sgt. Skinner and L/Cpl. Radley of D Coy. 4th Essex Home Guard for their gallant conduct when a He 111 crashed at Hornchurch on 1/11/40. The blazing machine descended near to the entrance of an Anderson shelter in which three people were trapped. Armed with shovels, the men burrowed to the entrance and, despite the fact that their clothing took fire, they handed out a man, woman and child. Sgt. Skinner freed people trapped in another shelter and was burned about the hands and face. Despite the courage of the Home Guards the three persons rescued from the first shelter succumbed to their injuries.

G1+KN, an He111 H-4 of 5./KG55 was one of the force attacking Bristol on 24 November, 1940. The bomber received a direct hit from anti aircraft fire and exploded before crashing into the sea 300 yards off Rame, Head, Devon. The pilot, Oberfeldwebel Werner Müller and his three crew were killed, as was the war correspondent Emil Weihmüller.

Oberfeldwebel Werner Müller

On 8 December He111 P-2 G1+LT of 9./KG55 crashed taking off from Villacoublay bound for London. All four of the crew perished in the accident, left to right: Unteroffizier Heinz Herrmann, Feldwebel Karl Reis, and Feldwebel Gottfried Schreier. (Margarete Reis)

The tail of G1+PL that fell in the garden of Underwood House, Etchingham, Sussex, on 22 December, 1940. It was shot down by Pilot Officer Benson and Sergeant Blain in a Defiant of 141 Squadron. Only the observer, Gefreiter Adolf Waibel, survived.

He111 P, Wn. 1992 was the survivor of many raids on Britain. Wearing the codes G1+HP of 6./KG55 and the highly individual tail graffiti, it was a regular mount of Gerhard Pulver, but was not the aircraft in which he was killed on 16 August, which also wore the codes G1+HP. (Magdalene Burmeier)

Stabsfeldwebel Karl Brüning, prisoner of war.

Oberfeldwebel Willi Weisse, died in the aircraft.

Merseyside was the target scheduled for 12 March 1941. He111 P-4 Wn. 2994, was being flown by Stabsfeldwebel Karl Brüning of 5./KG55 when it was intercepted over Sussex by Pilot Officer Hughes and gunner Sergeant Gash in a Defiant of No. 264 Squadron.

Gash picked up a Bandit at 800 yards, and about 700 feet above and flying on a parallel course on the port beam. This aircraft was approached under the-starboard wing and was identified as a Heinkel 111. It was engaged from 50, yards with a series of one second bursts, The first burst started a small fire in the starboard engine. At this stage the reflector sight failed. Sgt Gash carried on firing with night tracer and transferred the aim to the cabin area of the Heinkel. The de-Wilde ammunition could be seen bursting inside the cabin which filled with flames. The Bandit fell away to port in a spiral dive and struck the ground and exploded.

Combat Report.
Pilot Officer Hughes No. 264 Squadron.

Feldwebel Alexander Düssel, killed when his parachute failed.

Feldwebel Konrad Steiger, died in the aircraft.

"I was surprised by the many direct hits. The machine caught fire and both motors were hit, they stopped at once. I lost height quickly. Through the intercom I heard screaming and groaning of both my comrades, wireless operator Steiger and flight mechanic Weisse, who seemed to be heavily wounded. My left hand and left anklebone were hit, but my back and seat were protected by an 8mm armour plate. I felt only a light blow. I had no pain. I gave Düssel the order to crawl to the back to open the escape hatch and get our two comrades out. Whether they were dead or wounded I could not know, but it was their only chance. Düssel came back and said that he could not reach them as the gangway was already on fire. I gave the order 'Ready to jump'. Düssel immediately jumped out through the side hatch. I found out later that his parachute did not open."

Karl Brüning

G1+CP an He111 P-4 of 6./KG55 was also brought down on the Merseyside raid of 12 March, 1941. It was intercepted over Widnes by Sergeant McNair in a Hurricane of 96 Squadron. Hauptman Wolfgang Berlin (Staffelkapitän) was one of the three men to bale out safely.

After being attacked by MacNair, the Heinkel hit a barrage balloon cable. These men of Site 1, No. 922 (Balloon) Squadron RAF, were happy to believe that 'their' balloon was the victor. (Maddock)

"It was about 23.30 hours, and my faithful He111, the Gl+CP, had just dropped her bomb load on the target. I was about to close the bomb doors, when all at once there was a terrific crashing and banging in the aircraft and I saw tracer bullets flying past the cockpit left and right. A night fighter had got on to us, nothing to boast of, considering that there was a brilliant full moon. The right engine packed up at once and the left followed suit as the night fighter flew at us for the third time. We were losing height and the right engine began to smoke So I gave the order: 'Jump for it!'. But only the pilot, the W/T operator and I were able to do so, the mechanic and the rear gunner lay dead at their posts. We discovered later that the former had his spine shattered and the latter had a bullet through the head.

"We baled out at about 3,000 feet and I seemed to be hovering over England in complete immobility. I saw the light of the explosion when the Heinkel crashed, and then realised that I should have to be careful if I did not want to be left hanging in a high tension cable. I curled up my legs and was over it, and a moment later landed with a bump in a field. I stood alone in the moonlight thanking heaven I had once again been spared, and thought of my wife, who would be so long without news of me. Then a young boy approached circumspectly and directly afterwards two older men, who took me along to a nearby farm, where the farmer's wife offered me tea, which I accepted. I ate a few biscuits with my tea, and with the wrapping I burnt some other papers which I did not propose that the English should have. Soon the room was filled with Air Raid Wardens and Home Guardsmen, who were anxious to gape at a German airman and to collect souvenirs. But I had nothing to give them."

Hauptman Wolfgang Berlin

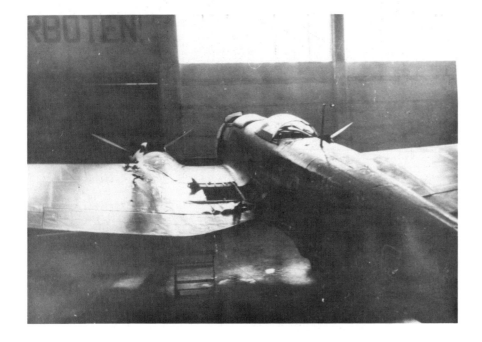

On the night of 13/14 March, 1941, Oberfeldwebel Bernhard Hickel's 8./KG55 Heinkel was attacked by a night fighter over the south coast of England. Feldwebels Herbert Schloms and Fritz Drechsel were injured and the port wing was set alight. Hickel safely landed G1+GS at Le Bourget. (Hickel)

The damage to the port wing of G1+GS. (Hickel)

Oberfeldwebel Bernhard Hickel. (Hickel)

Feldwebel Herbert Schloms. (Hickel)

Unteroffizier Robert Ehlers, gunner. (Sturat via Irwin)

Unteroffizier Hans Wagner, pilot. (Irwin)

Oberleutnant Hans-Ludwig Wolff, observer. (Irwin)

Oberleutnant Hans-Ludwig Wolff was the observer aboard G1+IR on a sea reconnaissance sortie off the English southwest coast on 2 April, 1941. Wolff had trained as an observer in pre-war years and had been posted to 7./KG55 shortly before Christmas. The Heinkel was intercepted by Flight Lieutenant Parsons in a Hurricane from No. 504 Squadron and crashed into the sea two miles south of Budleigh Salterton, Devon. Wolff's was the only body recovered from the sea, the other men were never found.

Oberfeldwebel Heinrich Schwiering was the pilot of G1+KH of 1./KG55 engaged on a sortie to Greenock, Scotland, on 8 April 1941. He was intercepted by Pilot Officer Hodgkinson and Sergeant Dye in a Beaufighter of No. 219 Squadron. The Heinkel fell into the sea off Worthing, Sussex, killing all four crewmen.

On 9 April, 1941, fourteen aircraft of I./KG55 took part in a raid on Coventry. G1+DL (above) was brought down by Pilot Officer Stevens DFC in a Hurricane of No. 151 Squadron at Roes Rest Farm, Peckleton, Leicestershire. All four crew, including flight engineeer Feldwebel Herbert Link (left) were taken prisoner. Link was still aboard the aircraft when it crashed. He was unconscious for three months and in hospital for a year before being sent to a prison camp. In 1943 Link was repatriated and joined a Luftwaffe fighter unit on the Russian front. The observer aboard G1+DL was Hauptman Otto Bodemeyer, the Gruppenkommandeur I./KG55. (Thea Link)

Mr Fowler, owner of Roe's Rest Farm, looked out of his window when he heard the noise of the crashing Heinkel and discovered that one of his trees had been replaced by the wreckage of the bomber.

G1+LS Wn. 2808 (above) crashed in Windsor Great Park, Berkshire, on 9 April, 1941. The aircraft had been intercepted by Flight Lieutenant McMullen DFC and Bar in a Defiant of No. 151 Squadron. G1+LS had a small shield painted on the starboard side of the fin. The emblem came from the German expression 'small fish' meaning no problem, and became the emblem of III./KG55.

Oberleutenant Jürgen Bartens.

Feldwebel Hermann Kübler.

Oberfeldwebels Franz Vonier and Fritz Pons.

The three fish emblem worn by Wn. 2808.

G1+DN lies broken at Lodge Bottom, Busbridge, Surrey, on 9 April, 1941. The pilot, Unteroffizier Alfred Muller, attempted to make a landing after being attacked by Flight Sergeant Thorn in a Defiant of No. 264 Squadron. The aircraft crashed through trees that tore off the wings and smashed the nose of the bomber, where three of the four men died.

On 15/16, April a strange event took place in the skies over south Wales. G1+DS of 8./KG55 was attacked by a night fighter that disabled both engines and set the bomber alight. Three of the crew baled out and were taken into captivity, they were: Unteroffizier Herbert Czaplinski, Obergefreiter Heinrich Schmidt, and Gefreiter Hubert Häffner who spent the night hanging by his parachute in a tree. The pilot, Feldwebel Fritz Költsch, regained control and returned to Villacoubley.

KG55 in captivity. Back row, left to right, Fritz Pons (PoW 9 April 1941), Herbert Sauer (PoW 16 April 1941), unknown, unknown, Heinrich Schmidt (PoW 15 April 1941). Front row, Hubert Häffner (PoW 15 April 1941), Herbert Czaplinski (PoW 15 April 1941), unknown, Horst Rosenberg (PoW 16 April 1941), Herman Kübler (PoW 9 April 1941). (Pons)

Belfast was the target for 15/16 April, 1941, when G1+ES Wn. 2857 of 8./KG55 was shot down by Squadron Leader John Cunningham in a Beaufighter of No. 604 Squadron. Cannon shells from the Beaufighter destroyed the controls of the Heinkel and the cockpit filled with smoke. Pilot, Oberleutnant Gunther von Seidlitz, and his crew, baled out but his parachute failed to deploy properly and he was killed. Observer, Feldwebel Franz Hümmer's parachute became entangled in a barrage balloon cable and he fell to his death. Unteroffiziers Herbert Sauer and Horst Rosenberg landed safely and were taken prisoner.

The remains of G1+ES in Padwell Road, Southampton. (Southern Newspapers Ltd)

The bodies of Oberleutnant Günther von Seidlitz and Feldwebel Franz Hümmer were buried in Stoneham Cemetery, Southampton. (Southern Newspapers Ltd)

On the night of 4/5 May, 1941, crews of KG55 flew sorties to three targets: Belfast, and two locations in the Liverpool area. He111 P-4 Wn. 2942 G1+GM of 4./KG55 crashed after taking off from Chartres at La Ferté Vidame. The four crew were killed. They were: Gefreiter Karl Decker, pilot, Gefreiter Gerhard Christoph, Observer, Gefreiter Heinz Reichert, wireless operator, Gefreiter Franz Perzinger, Flight Engineer.

Major Dr. Ernst Kühl, Gruppenkommandeur II./KG55, pays his respects to one of his crews at Chartres. After the war they were reinterred in Solers Cemetery, Melun. (Haase)

KG55 suffered four losses on 7/ 8 May, 1941. The target was again Liverpool.

G1+LH of 1./KG55 fell at Torkington Golf Club, Hazel Grove, Cheshire. It had been shot down by Flight Lieutenant Deanesly in a Defiant of No. 256 Squadron. The crew of four all took to their parachutes and were captured. (Ron Collier)

Leutnant Günther Becker.

Leutnant Günther Becker was the pilot of G1+GH from 1./KG55. All four crew and the Heinkel disappeared without trace in curcumstances that have never been explained. (Walter Schmid)

G1+KL crashed into the sea off Portland, Dorset, and all five of the crew were killed. Four bodies were found on 13 May (six days later) and a rubber dinghy was found nearby. It was reported that the bodies had been 'in the water only a matter of hours' and death was due to drowning. What became of the men is a mystery, as in six days the bodies and boat would have drifted apart and certainly be in a far worse condition than the report would seem to indicate. The body of Unteroffizier Willibald Amann was buried at the Naval Cemetery, Portland, with his three comrades.

The fourth loss was G1+HP from 6./KG55, which crashed near Wrexham, Denbighshire. The four crewmen were killed when the bomber exploded in the air and disintegrated. It had been intercepted by Flight Lieutenant West in a Defiant of No. 256 Squadron.

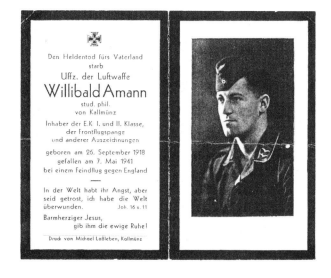

Colin North and Dennis Clayton, members of C Company 5th Royal Warwick Home Guard, pose with the wreck of G1+MT at Fulford Hall Farm, south of Birmingham. Oberleutnant Johannes Speck von Sternberg, Staffelkapitän 9./KG55, and two others were killed in the crash on 10/11 May, 1941. Gefreiter Rudolf Budde managed to bale out of the flaming bomber and was captured, but suffered terrible burns. It was reported shot down by Lewis gun fire from Lance Bombardier A. A. Hanson from the 380th Battery, 45th Searchlight Regiment, Royal Artillery.

KG55 lost five bombers on 10/11 May, 1941. In addition to G1+MT (above) G1+AR, G1+KR and G1+CK all vanished into the North Sea. G1+BT (left) was shot down at Balls Green, near Crowborough, Sussex. Two other aircraft returned damaged by gunfire.

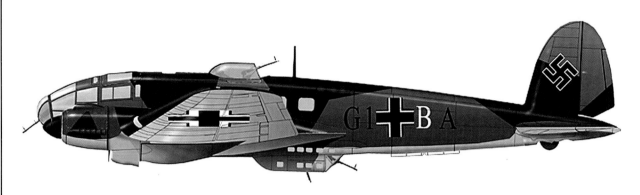

Heinkel He111P, G1+BA, of the Geschwader Stab KG55. This aircraft was being flown by John-Christian Mohn when it was slightly damaged by AA fire over Poland on 7th September 1939. The fuselage codes are peculiar to this early period of the war. (Photographic reference page 7).

Staffel emblem of 1/KG55

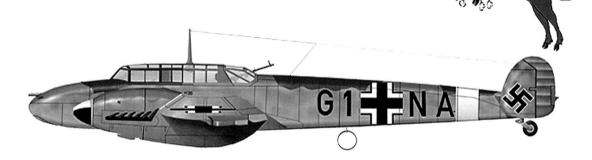

Messerschmitt Bf110C, G1+NA, operated by the Stab/KG55, France 1940-41. The aircraft is shown in a scheme of 02/71 over 65, with 02/71 mottling. Note the half and half black and white spinners.

Emblem of 2/KG55

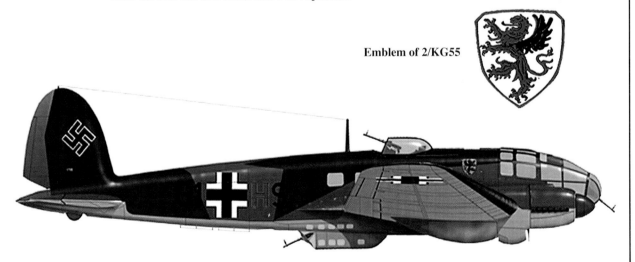

Heinkel He111P-2, G1+HS, Wk.Nr.1705 of 8/KG55. Unteroffizier Horst Mahnert strayed into Swiss air space on 2 June 1940, and was shot down by a Swiss air force Bf109 of 15 Fliegerkompanie. (Photographic reference page 11).

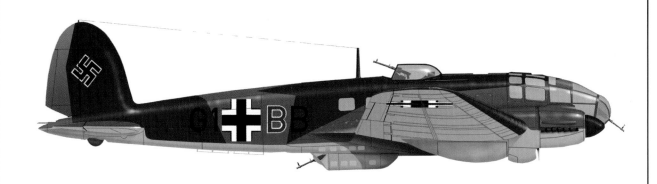

Heinkel He111P-2, G1+BB, of Stab I/KG55. After crash landing in Sussex on 26 August 1940, the RAF Air Intelligence Officer noted that the aircraft was fitted with an MG15 to fire out of the tail and that the first 'B' of the codes was painted in red with a white border. (Photographic reference page 24).

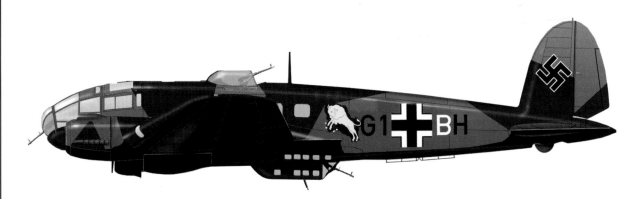

Heinkel He111H-2, G1+BH, Wk.Nr.6305 of 1/KG55. Fw. Fritz Jurges was forced to crash land this Heinkel, on the 25th September 1940, near Swanage, in Dorset. The white bull was the Staffel emblem and the undersides were painted lamp-black in preparation for night operations, although the aircraft was lost on a daylight raid. (Photographic reference page 28).

Heinkel He111P-2, G1+HP, Wk.Nr.1992 of 6/KG55. The survivor of many raids on Britain and adorned with highly individual tail graffiti, this was one of several KG55 Heinkels known to have worn the code G1+HP. (Photographic reference page 37).

The crew of G1+ES of 8./KG55 was briefed for a special 'free-lance' operation, on 11/12 May, 1941. The night watchman aboard the Short S.21 'Maia' composite flying boat G-ADHK, moored in Poole Harbour, Dorset, is believed to have been showing a red light that was spotted by the Heinkel crew. Feldwebel Willy Wimmer went down to investigate and attacked the flying boat with gunfire. 'Maia' sank, taking the night watchman to his death in its nose. The Heinkel returned over the harbour a few minutes later and was hit by anti aircraft fire from shipping. The bomber hit the sea and exploded.

Feldwebel Heinrich Neuber, wireless operator, was found dead at Poole Quay. (Hickel)

Unteroffizier Karl Scheuringer, was thrown out of the wreck and was captured. (Scheuringer)

The tail section of G1+GR that was shot down during a sortie to Birmingham on 17 May, 1941. The Heinkel was intercepted by Pilot Officer Hodgkinson DFC in a Beaufighter of 219 Squadron, and broke up in the air north of Worthing, Sussex. Leutnant Helmut Pichler and his crew of three were all killed.

Gefreiter Josef Wiederer, gunner, buried at sea. (Max Wiederer)

Feldwebel Lorenz Kempel, observer, buried at sea. (Wilhelm Kempel)

Feldwebel Otto Stadel, flight engineer, found at Padstow. (Alois Stadel)

KG55's last loss of the 'Blitz' was an He111 H-8, Wn.3867, G1+AM of 4./KG55. The crew was engaged on an armed reconnaissance on 27 May, 1941, when they were intercepted by Spitfires from No. 66 Squadron and shot down into the sea off Gurnards Head, Cornwall. All five of the crew were killed.

In mid June, 1941, orders arrived to Luftwaffe units in the West detailing movement orders:

12 June, 1941, I Gruppe KG 55 move from Melun/Villaroche aerodrome, south of Paris, France, to Labunie aerodrome, south east of Zamosz, Poland.
17 June, 1941, the Geschwaderstab KG 55 move from Villacoublay aerodrome, south of Paris, to Labunie aerodrome, south east of Zamosz, Poland.
18, June, 1941, II Gruppe KG 55 move from Chartres Aerodrome, SW of Paris, to Labunie aerodrome, south east of Zamosz, Poland.
18, June, 1941, III Gruppe KG 55 moved from Villacoublay aerodrome to Klemensow aerodrome, west of Zamooz, south east of Lublin, Poland.

The Erganzungstaffel based at Landsberg aerodrome, Near Munich, became IV Gruppe KG55 on 8 March, 1941. On 21 March it moved to Dijon/Longvic aerodrome, France, where it was to remain until 4 May, 1944.

Russia -Operation Barbarossa

The Operational Area for KG55 in the Russian Campaign

Kursk
Kursk

Stalingrad
Volgograd

Kiew
Kiev

Charkow
Kharkov

Morosowskaja
Morozovsk

Pitomnik

Shitomir
Zhitomir

Poltawa
Poltava

Kirowograd
Kirovograd

Stalino
Donetsk

Ukraine

Sea of Azov

Kertsch
Kerch

Noworossisk
Novorossiysk

Crimea

Caucasus Mountains

Sewastopol
Sevastopol

Black Sea

One of KG55's Heinkels over Russia, displaying the yellow fuselage band and wing tips. KG55 lost seven aircraft and crews on the opening day of Operation Barbarossa, 22 June 1941. The operations were in support of Field Marshal von Rundstedt's Army Group South.

The airfiel at Labunie, home of Stab, I, and II Gruppen in June and July, 1941. The Gruppen moved rapidly between Labunie, Shitomir and Bojary during the first two months of the Russian campaign.

The accommodation at Shitomir, August 1941.

Feldwebel Schmidt and Unteroffizier Wirsch at Bojary airfield, July 1941.

G1+KS of 8./KG55 was shot down by Flak 40Km west of Luck, on 23 June, 1941. The crew baled out, but met their deaths at the hands of the Russians. Feldwebel Otto Henkis, Leutnant Freidrich Raschka, and Oberfeldwebel Paul Brzoska were found shot through their heads and hearts. Feldwebel Hermann Moeller and Unteroffizier Adolf Hubbert were found in the house of the local Commissar; shot in the back of their heads.

This He111 of 5./KG55 was forced to crash land after being hit by Flak on 16 July, 1941.

On this occasion the crew would appear to be on good terms with the Russian civilians and enjoying an impromptu picnic!

The He111 H-6 was the standard equipment of the Heinkel units in Russia. In addition to KG55, KG27, KG53 and KG4 were operational Heinkel Geschwadern in Russia, but by August 1941, they had only 128 servicable aircraft between them.

SC1000 bombs and other ordnance are readied for this III./KG55 machine identified by the three fish painted on the rudder.

One of the Heinkels undergoing engine maintenance. During the summer of 1941, the German forces pushed all before them and KG55 moved eastwards, towards Stalingrad and the Caucasus oilfields.

Robert Seib at the controls of his 6./KG55 He111. Seib had a remarkable career in KG55. In October 1941 he completed 100 missions, on 9 October 1943 he was awarded the Ritterkreuz as Oberleutnant and Staffelkapitan 6./KG55 with 330 missions. At the war's end he had survived 488 missions.

A battered Heinkel whose markings have become indecipherable under the mud which has splashed up the fuselage sides.

A 20mm Flakvierling 38 Sd. Kfz. 7/1 half-track used to defend KG55's airfields against Russian bombers.

By November 1941 the German advance had stalled against stronger Russian defense and counter attacks. Stab KG55 and I, II and III Gruppe had been at Kirowograd in the Ukraine for up to three months.

Standard equipment of the Wehrmacht, the Panzer III, overflown by a Storch used to recover downed aircrew.

View from the accommodation block in Kirowograd. In October 1941 home to I, II and III Gruppen KG55.

A Petlyakov Pe-2 found near Kiew in 1941. The majority of missions were flown against Russian forces in the Charkow region, an area in the Ukraine that was fought over and changed hands many times in three years.

A wrecked T-34 found near Morosowskaja. The T-34 was the most successful of the Russian tanks and made its first appearance in the defence of Moscow in late 1941.

The slow moving T-35, a design of the mid 1930s, was a leviathon that proved no match for the German forces that have climbed aboard this one.

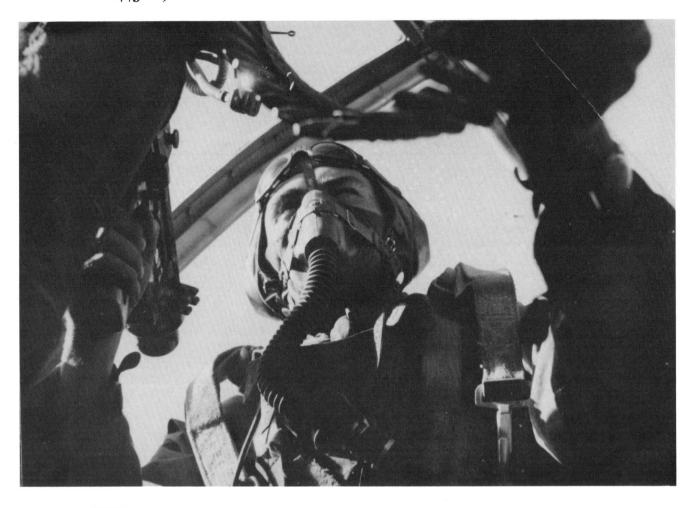

Feldwebel Meisel at his position as wireless operator aboard Leutnant Luxenburger's G1+CM of 4./KG55.

Oberleutnant Josef Luxenburger and his crew. Feldwebel Ruhnau (gunner), Feldwebel Buchheister (engineer), Oberleutnant Koller (Staffelkapitan and pilot), Leutnant Luxenburger (observer), Feldwebel Meisel (wireless operator).

A Tupolev SB-2 bis bomber discovered in the Crimea.

Otto Gabenstätter, Rheinhard Haase and Andreas Rumpmaier of 4./KG55 pose with a captured Russian ANT-4 bomber built in the mid 1930s. The annotation reveals their opinion of the aircraft!

Heinkels of 3./KG55 in formation on their way to Melun-Villaroche for the winter.

Willi Dölker. In the winter of 1941/42 KG55 moved west, away from the Russian Front. The Stab moved to Evreux from November 1941 to April 1942. I Gruppe moved to Melun-Villaroche from October to December 1941, II Gruppe was at St Andre From November to April, and III Gruppe went to Nantes also from November 1941 to April 1942.

Unteroffier Georg Haan, Unteroffizier Gerhard Dietrich, Unteroffizier Rheinhard Haase, Obergerfreiter Andreas Rumpmaier, Unteroffizier Ernst Günther of 4./KG55. Dietrich was awarded the Ritterkreuz on 9 June 1944 and completed 436 missions by the end of the war.

Stalemate in the East

All units with the exception of IV Gruppe had returned to the Ukraine by the end of April 1942. The German 11th Army was besieging Sewastopol and 6th Army was involved in battle in the Charkow area where the front line moved back and forth until the 6th Army took control in June.

Kertch, key to the siege of Sewastopol, was captured in May and Field Marshal von Manstein's 11th Army took Sebastopol itself on 3 July. On 23 July Hitler ordered simultaneous attacks on the Caucasus and Stalingrad. On the night of 23/24 August KG55 took part in the 'maximum effort' attack on Stalingrad that resulted in 40,000 people being killed in the conflagration. III Gruppe lost one of its crews, the Geschwader's only casualty that night.

Wounded troops were transported from the Charkow front to air-fields where KG55 was based. This aircraft carried the codes L5+BB, from Stab I./Kampfgruppe z.b.V.5.

A safe landing. The wooden propeller blades on the port engine have been shattered, but only the lower blade on the starboard engine is broken, indicating that failure of the starboard engine caused the crash landing. (Martin Junglehner).

Hauptman Rybka of 5./KG55 flew the 4000th mission on 24 April, 1942. Note the badge of 5 Staffel.

The Samara bridge at Noworossisk on the south coast of the Caucasus.

Stalingrad

In November Russian forces counter-attacked and surrounded the 6th Army at Stalingrad. Göring told Hitler that the Luftwaffe could supply the Army from the air. Ju52s and He111s bore the brunt of this.

A Polikarpov Po-2 'Sewing Machine' used for nuisance raids over airfields near front line.

The remains of a Yak 1 fighter. While the battle for Stalingrad was grinding on, the Russians pushed the German forces back in the Fourth Battle of Charkow, which was re-captured on 26 March 1943.

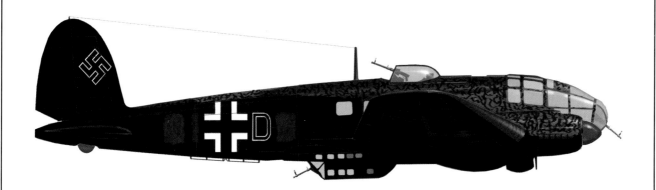

Heinkel He111P-2, G1+DN, Wk.Nr. 1423 of 5/KG55. The RAF Air Intelligence IA1(g) reported on this Heinkel found at Busbridge, Surrey, on 9 April 1941. It had night camouflage and a grenade ejector tube in the tail, the 'D' of the code was black with a white edge, and the spinners were red, the correct staffel colour. (Photographic reference page 44).

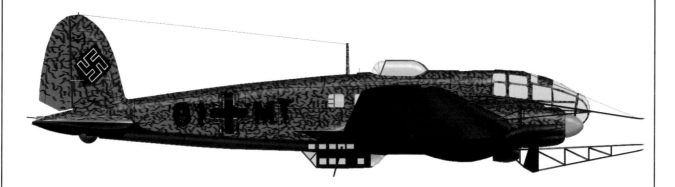

Heinkel He111H-8, G1+MT, Wk.Nr. 3971 of 9/KG55. Wearing a different night camouflage pattern and carrying a balloon defender before it, the Heinkel of Oblt. Speck von Sternberg crashed near Birmingham on 10 May 1941. Although badly damaged, the camouflage and markings were noted: Upper surfaces daubed lamp black, lamp black undersides, swastikas and lettering obliterated, yellow spinners. An MG17 was fitted in the tail. (photographic reference page 48).

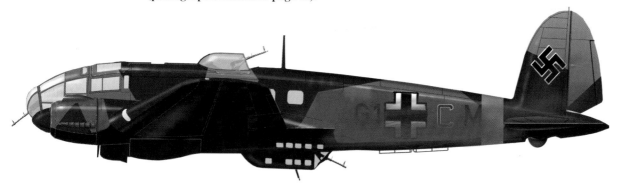

Heinkel He111H-8, G1+CM, of 4/KG55. Typical of the Heinkels used in Operation Barbarossa, this gives a good idea of the conditions that the Luftwaffe was forced to operate under. (Photographic reference page 55).

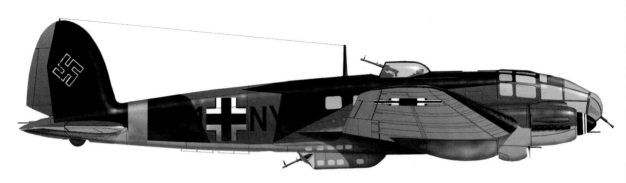

Heinkel He111H-16, G1+NY, of 14.(Eis)/KG55. He111's of this unit were
fitted with six forward firing 20mm cannon to attack railway targets in
Russia. (Photographic reference page 78).

Emblem of 8/KG55.

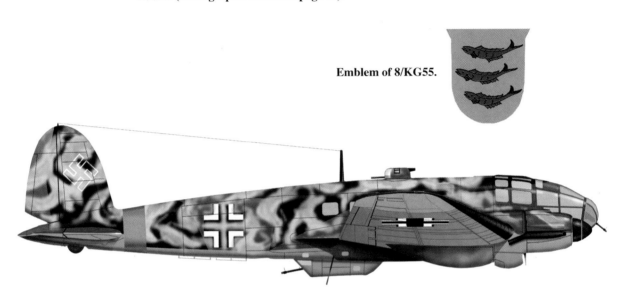

He111H-20/R3. One of the last variants of Heinkel's design, it was fitted
with a 13mm MG131 dorsal turret that was remotely operated. During winter
operations in 1944, a wave camouflage scheme was applied by the unit in the
field. (Photographic reference page 79).

Emblem of I./KG55. Originally that
of KGrzbV5.

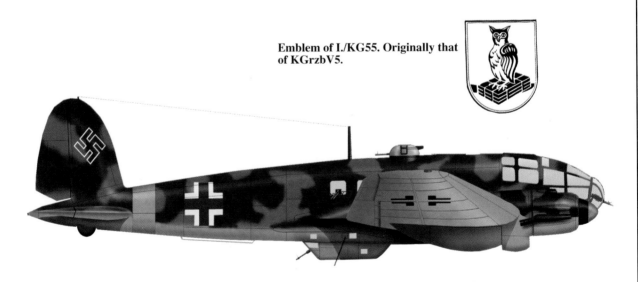

Heinkel He111H-20 of III/KG55. Typical of the last Heinkels operated by
KG55, this has the MG81Z 'twin' machine guns in the fuselage, and the
camouflage is completely different to earlier schemes. (Photographic
reference page 81).

On 14 January 1943 Pitomnik airfield was captured by the Russians. This had been a vital base for the Stalingrad airlift, so many supplies had to be parachuted in. The last 40,000 German troops surrendered on 2 February. The German losses at Stalingrad had been 110,500 killed, 50,000 wounded and 107,500 taken prisoner. The Russians lost 750,000 troops and 250,000 civilians killed. The Luftwaffe lost 266 Ju52s, 165 He111s, 42 Ju86s, 9 FW200s, 5 He177s and a single Ju290 in the air lift. KG55 lost 59 aircraft, but evacuated 9,161 troops from November to the fall of Stalingrad.

Pre-heating the engines was vital in the winter when temperatures fell to minus 30 degrees Centigrade.

The 250,000 men of the 6th Army only received 90 tonnes of bread and other supplies a day.

Stab I./Kampfgruppe zbV5 joined KG55 in the supply drops. L5+BB was damaged by an attacking Russian fighter, but returned safely to Stalino.

The badge of Kampfgruppe z.b.V.5 on a motorcycle combination. On 1 May 1943, the entire I Gruppe KG55 became III./LG1 and moved to Barth. Kampfgruppe z.b.V.5 was re-designated I./KG55 based at Stalino on the same day.

Franz Boehm and G. Willotzski
after they both received the Iron
Cross 2nd Class. Willotzski was
killed at Bengasi in North Africa
in November 1943.

Oberfeldwebel Suppmeyer of 5./KG55 received a
rather large Iron Cross.

The main Luftwaffe cemetery
at Saki in the Crimea.

Friesacher was killed by cannon
fire in G1+RK of 2./KG55.

II./KG55 celebrate their 10,000th feindflug on 11 May 1943. The Gruppenkommandeur was Major Heinrich Höfer who received the Ritterkreuz on 14 September 1943 and the Eichenlaub on 18 November 1944 after flying 546 missions.

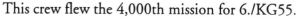

This crew flew the 4,000th mission for 6./KG55.

Leutnant Wolfgang Glieden.

The Long Road to Defeat

Leutnant Anton Brandauer of 2./KG55.
Army operations ground to a halt in the spring thaw, but Hitler was planning Operation Zitadelle, the summer offensive at Kursk.

Becker, Junglehner, Kumpler, and Britsch. In June 1943 Feldwebel Martin Junglehner joined 14.(Eisenbahnbekämpfungsstaffel)/KG55, a specialist unit developed to fly at very low level to attack Russian trains. Unteroffizier Bruno Britsch was killed on 11 June 1943 during a railway attack.

Kurt Baumann and his wireless operator Kaden.

Oberleutnant Hermann Meyer of Stab II./KG55 was the only crewman killed when G1+AC was shot down near Anapa on 6 May 1943. Anapa was a key location on the southern Caucasus.

Most cemeteries such as this one were destroyed by the Russians following their advance.

Oberfeldwebel Willi Nemitz, holder of the Ritterkreuz, was killed on 10 April 1943.

Twenty year old Franz Weinert of 8./KG55 flew 120 missions in 10 weeks during the autumn of 1943.

Werke No. 110076 shows some unusual paint weathering and carries the small G1 marking of the late war schemes. The fairing at the bottom of the tail has been removed and it would appear that the tail wheel has collapsed.

Crews of 5./KG55 prepare for another mission in the autumn of 1943. (Fritz Bohmichen).

Bernd Roski (gunner), Walter Dietrich (engineer), Hans Breit (radio operator), Hans Caro (pilot), Robert Sellner (observer), and their ground mechanic.

Hans Caro was forced to crash land on 23 September 1943 after an attack on Bolschoi-Tokmak in the Ukraine. The Heinkel sustained severe damage.

Robert Sellner (observer), Hans Caro (pilot), and Hans Breit (radio operator) celebrate their 200th mission with a bottle of champagne.

Franz Boehm took a series of photographs during his time with 2./KG55. These images are from his album.

The 20mm cannon mounting in the nose of the He111 H series.

Morosowskaja railway station, where I./KG55 was based for the whole of 1943.

Franz Boehm's He111 H-6.

The photographer, sitting on an SC1000 bomb.

The crew pose for a snap by their G1+EK.

Aircraft of 7./KG55 in formation. The nearest aircraft, G1+LR, flown by Hans Unmack was damaged by Russian fighters on 3 October 1943 and forced to land.

Hans Unmack at the contols of his Heinkel, with his observer Puttich at his side.
In the second half of 1943 Russian forces pushed back the Germans 300Km across the Ukraine.

Unteroffizier Hans Dengler gunner), Unteroffizier Jupp Remus (observer), Feldwebel Egon Buschgen (pilot), Unteroffizier Martin Winkler (wireless operator).

The griffon badge continues to be carried on KG55's Heinkels. This one is from 9./KG55. As the Russian forces over-ran the airfields, KG55 was forced to join the retreat.

Rheinhard Haase, Leutnant Berking, Gerhard Dietrich, Hauptmann Schmittmann, Otto Gabestatter, Andreas Rumpmaier, George Haan after completing 300 missions. Note the damage to the port aileron.

Ritterkreuz holder Oberleutnant Josef Luxenburger after his 500th mission on 12 November 1943. His engineer, Oberfeldwebel Buchheister completed 400 missions.

This rare photograph shows an He111 H-16 used by 14.(Eis)/KG55 the specialist train-busting unit. It has been fitted with six forward firing 20mm cannon. He111s of this unit were fitted with an electronic alitmeter that allowed them to fly at only 20 metres above the tracks. The Staffel lost nine crews but flew over 5,000 missions.

Despite the superiority of the their equipment, the German forces suffered defeat after defeat in the winter of 1943/44.

He111 H-20/R3 flown by Feldwebel Egon Burschlen. This was one of the last variants of Heinkel's design and was fitted with a 13mm MG131dorsal turret that was remotely operated.

Bombing up of a winter camouflaged Heinkel on the last day on 1943, Russian forces over-ran Shitomir, one of KG55's earlier airfields

Winter camouflaged He111 H-16s in the winter of 1943/44.

Major Richard Brunner, was Gruppenkommandeur I./KG55 until his promotion to Geschwaderkommodore on 22 November 1944. He held this position until 8 May 1945, the day after the German surrender.

On 10 May, 1944, KG55 flew its 50,000th mission. Kommodore Willi Antrup was there to greet the crew on returning from Schepetowka railway station.

The senior officers of KG55 together. Oberstleutnant Wilhelm Antrup (Geschwaderkommodore), Major Richard Brunner (Kommandeur I Gruppe), Major Alfred Bollmann (Kommandeur II Gruppe), Major Heinz Hofer (Kommandeur III Gruppe). The photograph was taken on New Year's Day 1944 in Poland.

Wireless operator / gunner Unteroffizier Heiner Blanz and his He111 H-20 of III/KG55. This has the MG81Z 'twin' machine guns in the fuselage.

Unteroffizier Heiner Blanz wearing his bronze war flight badge and EKII insignia.

Leutnant Glieden of 9./KG55 in the summer of 1944.

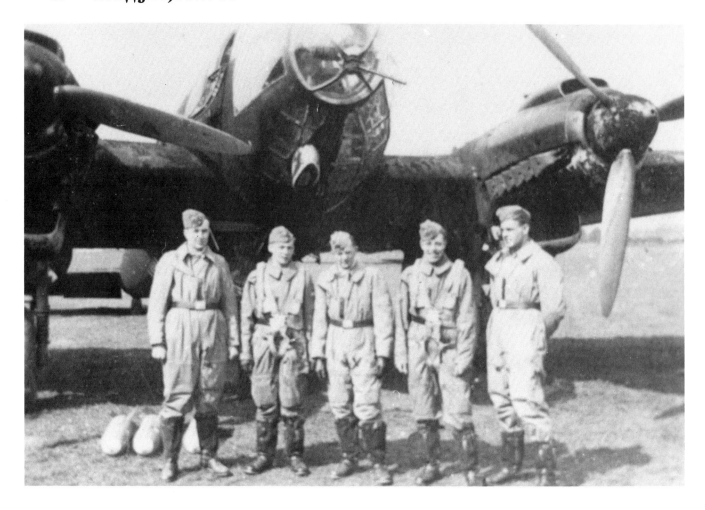

IV./KG55 Operations in the West

While I, II, and III Gruppen of KG55 were committed to operations on the Russian Front, IV./KG55 remained in the west until May 1944. During that time the unit took part in a small number of missions against Britain in addition to their training role.

G1+GV, Stab IV./KG55 was en-route to Birmingham when shot down by a Beaufighter from No.604 Squadron on 30/31 July 1942. The He111 H-6 crashed near Weymouth, Dorset, killing three of its crew including Ritterkreuz holder Hauptmann Karbe who had flown over 250 missions. Oberfeldwebel Bock was captured on his 235th mission. (Heading photo shows Richard Bock, centre, with his crew in front of his He111 H-6).

Hauptmann Adelbert Karbe.

Oberfeldwebel Richard Bock.

Kampfgeschwader 55

Greif

This card was made to celebrate the 207th mission of Leutnant Keinpkens crew. The crew had been shot down three times and in 1943 were based at Dijon.

Beobachter
Uffz. K. Meier
✝ 28.8.1943

Bordmechaniker
Feldwebel
Wilh. Wazek

Flugzeugführer
Leutnant
H. Keinpkens

Bordfunker
Unteroffz.
R. Auhagen

Bordschütze
Obergefreiter
Peter Huber

Leutnant Willi Dölker (left) of IV./KG55 flying from Dijon before moving to the Russian front.

On 23 April, 1944, five Mustangs from No.122 Squadron attacked Dole/Tavaux airfield, near Dijon and claimed to have shot down six He111s and damaged a Gotha Go242 and a further He111.

Above and left, G1+MU flown by Hans Langbehn was hit at least 78 times. Unteroffizier Kurt Dege at one time had a Mustang in his gunsight, but had forgotten to turn on the power supply required to fire the gun.

Hans Langbehn, pilot of G1+MU with his old wireless operator Gefreiter Gastreich. Paul Gastreich was among many KG55 personnel badly burned when a phosphorous bomb fell on an air-raid shelter during a raid Dijon airfield on 28 March 1944.

G1+CX from 13./KG55 was another victim of the 23 April raid. One crewman was seriously injured. (Guy Coquillat)

Wing Commader G.H. Goodman DSO, DFC and Flying Officer W.F.E. Thomas of No.151 Squadron after their return from Dijon on 4 May 1944. Four He111s of IV./ KG55 were claimed shot down. (Thomas).

Ritterkreuz Holders - KG55.

Major Alfrex Bollmann.

Oberleutnant Josef Luxenburger.

Leutnant Erich Herkner.

Feldwebel Walter Pilz.

Oberst Dr. Ernst Kühl.

Hauptmann Werner Schmidt.

Name	Unit	Date Awarded	Fate
Oberstleutnant Benno KOSCH	Kdr.II./KG 55	1.10.40	
Oberst Alois STOECKL	Kdore/KG 55	4.7.40	+14.8.40 England
Major Friedrich KLESS	Kdr.II./KG 55	14.10.40	
Oberleutnant Hans THURNER	FF. 9./KG 55	6.8.41	+11. 6.44 Normandy
Oberleutnant Adalbert KARBE	St.Kpt. 3./KG 55	12.11.41	+30. 7.42 England
Hauptmann Heinrich WITTMER	Kdr.III./KG 55	12.11.41	
Leutnant -Fritz BLIESENER	FF. 5./KG 55	20.12.41	+25.11.42 Russia
Hauptmann Rudolf KIEL	Kdr.I./KG 55	20.12.41	
Oberstleutnant Dr. Ernst KUHL	Kdore./KG 55	17.10.42	+2. 2.72
Oberleutnant Albert KOLLER	StKpt. 4./KG 55	13.11.42	
Hauptmann Wilhelm ANTRUP	StKpt. 5./KG 55	13.11.42	
Oberfeldwebel Karl LIPP	FF. 4/KG 55	16.11.42	+20.11.42 Stalingrad
Oberleutnant Eitel BARTH	StKpt. 4./KG 55	24.3.43	
Oberleutnant Horst RUDAT	StKpt. 2./KG 55	24.3.43	
Feldwebel Walter PILZ	FF. 5./KG 55	24.3.43	
Oberleutnant Werner OBERLÄNDER	StKpt. 2./KG 55	24.3.43	
Hauptmann Philipp MÜLLER	StKpt. 1./KG 55	3.4.43	
Oberfeldwebel Franz PLACZAK	FF.2./KG 55	3.4.43	
Oberleutnant Josef LUXENBURGER	BO. 4./KG 55	3.4.43	
Hauptmann Wilhelm MYLIUS	StKpt. 6./KG 55	3.4.43	+10. 9.70
Oberleutnant Brich BAUMGARTL	FF. 3./KG 55	31.7.43	+12.7.44 StKpt. 9./LG1
Oberleutnant Franz SCHMIDT	StKpt. 9./KG 55	19.8.43	+31.7.47
Major Heinz HÖFER	Kdr. III./KG 55	3.9.43	
Oberfeldwebel Johann BOOS	FF. 9./KG 55	9.10.43	PoW? 13.5.43
Oberleutnant Robert SEIB	StKpt. 6./KG 55	9.10.43	
Hauptmann Fritz SCHMIDTMANN	StKpt. 4./KG 55	29.2.44	
Oberfeldwebel Otto MEYER	FF. 14(Eis)./KG 55	29.2.44	+23.2.45 Eger

Oberleutnant Hans Bennemann.

Hauptmann Heinrich Wittmer.

Feldwebel Wilhelm Brennecke.

Leutnant Josef Thurnhuber.

Oberfeldwebel Johann Boos.

Oberleutnant M. Bermadinger.

Name	Unit	Date Awarded	Fate
Oberleutnant Hans BENNEMANN	FF. 7./KG 55	26.3.44	
Feldwebel Wilhelm BRENNECKE	FF. II./StabKG 55	26.3.44	
Oberleutnant Mathias BERMADING	FF. StKpt. 14(Eis)./KG 55	5.4.44	+18. 2.44 Pleskau
FahnenFeldwebel Willi BRAUN	BO. 4./KG 55	9.6.44	
Feldwebel Gerhard DIETRICH	FF. Stab./KG 55	9.6.44	
Hauptmann Werner SCHMIDT	StKpt. 9./KG 55	19.8.44	
Feldwebel Viktor KÖNIG	FF. 14(Eis).KG 55	6.10.44	+29.8.44 Russia
Oberleutnant Alfred VEITH	StKpt. 5./KG 55	24.10.44	
Oberleutnant, Werner THOSS	StKpt. 4./KG 55	29.10.44	
Major Alfred BOLLMANN	Kdr. III./KG 55	29.10.44	
Leutnant Erich HERKNER	FF. 14(Eis)./KG55	6.12.44	+17.1.45 Litzmannstadt
Hauptmann Alfred BANHOLZER	StKpt. 3./KG 55	14.1.45	
Feldwebel Karl SCHAFER	FF. 14(Eis)./KG55	3.4.45	
Hauptmann Oskar DETTKE	I./KG 55	7.4.45	+27.3.67
Oberleutnant Heinrich SÜDEL	Ia I./KG 55	23.4.45	
Ex KG55 Recipients			
Oberleutnant. Gerhard RICHTER	StKpt. 9./LG 1	24.11.40	
Generalmajor Wilhelm SÜSSMANN	Kdr. 7.Flg.Div.	9.7.41	+1941 Crete
Oberstleutnant Walter MARIENFELD	Kdore./KG 54	27.11.41	+24.10.44
Oberstleutnant Werner KLOSINSKI	Kdore./KG 4	9.6.44	
Oberleutnant, Günther JOLITZ	Stfhr. 9/LG 1	9.6.44	+12.2.44 Italy
Generalmajor Hans KORTE	Kdr. 2.Flg.Div.	30. 9.44	
Oberfeldwebel Herbert GEISLER	FF. Stab/KG 4	24.10.44	
Hauptm. D. C. von HOHENBERG	Kdr. II./LG 1	18.11.44	+30.6.44
Hauptmann Karl PETERS	Kdr. II./LG 1	1945	
Leutnant Josef THURNHUBER	FF. I./KG 200	12.3.45	
Leutnant Arnold DÖRING	FF. 10./NJG 3	17. 4.45	

KG55 Losses (In the West)

11 September 1939   He111   Stab KG 55
Oblt. Heinz Höfer and Uffz. Hans Siepen (67013/47) seriously wounded. Force landed between the lines at Przemysl, E of Krakow, Poland. The crew was rescued by German troops.

13 September 1939.   He111   Stab KG 55
Uffz. Karl Rathmann (67012/16) wounded.

14 September 1939.   He111   I./KG 55
Force landed Nr. Radow, SE of Warsaw, Poland.

15 September, 1939   He111   1/KG 55
Oblt. Walter Fritz (67015/2), Ofw. Josef Müller (67015/32), Uffz. Alfred Pientka (67015/48) and Ogfr. Siegfried Steinfurth (67015/45) killed. Chyrov, SW of L'vov, formerly Poland now in Russia.

10 May 1940.   He111   StabKG55
Fw. Karl Ander (67013/52), Fw. Karl Rathmann (67012/16) and Fw. Philipp Müller (67013/44), wounded. Toul - Epinal area of France.

12 May 1940   He111   4./KG55
G1+DM   (P) Ltn. Hans Junk (67019/93), (W) Uffz. Heinz Thöne (67019/32) (FE) Uffz. Wilhelm Ege (67019/40), and (G) Gfr. Harald Wendt (67019/70) killed. The sole survivor was (O) Uffz. Ernst Rasper (67019/27). Nr Rethel, NE of Reims, France.

12 May 1940   He111P   5./KG55
(FE) Uffz. Josef Bartholmes (67060/52) wounded. Attacked by fighters on return from Rethel, France.

13 May 1940   He111P   Stab KG55
G1+GA   (P) Oblt. Dieter Clemm von Hohenberg (67012/7), (W) Uffz. Hans Strobl (67013/112) and (G) Gfr. Franz Männer (67013/10) PoWs. (O) Fw. Willi Wolter (67013/29) and (FE) Ogfr. Hans Bell (67013/94) Killed. Vouziers, S of Charleville-Mézières, France.

13 May 1940   He 111   8./KG55
G1+HS   (P) Ofw. Bernhard Hickel (58246/238) and (O) Max Hausdörfer uninjured. (W) Gfr. Gerhard Arndt (58246/208), (FE) Fw. Willi,Herzog (58246/215) and (G) Gfr. Gustav Bodenhagen (58246/282) wounded. All returned to the German lines. Crash landed Nr. Vendresse 20 km S of Charleville- Mézières and was destroyed by the pilot and observer.

13 May 1940   He111   6./KG55
(P) Uffz. Heinrich Hänel (167018/28), (O) Ltn. Rudolf Bertelsmann (67015/44), (W) Uffz. Wilhelm Zierau (67018/24) and (FE) Uffz. Johannes Schmidt (67021/39) PoW. (G) Gfr. Josef Mittermaier (67021/92) killed. Charleville-Mézières, France.

13 May 1940   He111   6./KG55
(FE) Uffz. Max Stiller (67021/32) wounded by machine-gun fire.

13 May 1940   He111   StabII./KG55
Major Otto von Lachemair (67018/1) Gruppenkommandeur and Oberleutnant Siegfried Hensel (67018/4) Navigationsoffizier wounded by

AA. fire during operations against the railway station at Rethel, NE of Reims, France.

13 May 1940   He 111P   5./KG55
G1+FN   (P) Oberleutnant Gottfried Weigel (67020/4), (O) Fähnrich Ott, (FE) Unteroffizier Karl Gerdsmeier (67020/50) (W) Fw. Georg Engel (67020/37) and (G) Gefreiter Karl Geib (67020/84) all uninjured.
Attacked by 5 French Morane Saulnier MS 406s from astern. The attack damaged the port engine but the pilot force landed Nr Attert, N of Arlon, Belgium.

13 May 1940   He111   6./KG55
(P) Ltn. Horst Köhler (67021/5), (O) Fw. Paul Laufer (67019/18) and (W) Fw. Georg Engel (67021/28) PoW. (FE) Fw. Heinrich Winkelhaus (67021/23) and (G) Ogfr. Karl-Heinz Piur (67021/66) killed. Originally buried at Metz, N of Nancy, France.
As there were two Georg Engels in II/KG 55, Fw. Georg Engel (67021/28) was known as Engel 1 and Fw. Georg Engel (67020/37) was known as Engel 2.

13 May 1940   He111   6./KG55
(P) Ltn. Otto-Wilhelm Pöhler (67020/7) and (O) Ogfr. Fritz Höfling (67021/69) PoW. (W) Ogfr. Paul Brandt (67021/61), (FE) Uffz. Alois Freitag (67021/37) and (G) Gfr. Helmut Freiherr von Spiegel (67017/78) killed. Originally buried at Amblimont Cemetery, France.
Ltn. Pöhler was posted missing on 13 June 1943, with the rank of Hauptmann and Staffelkapitän of 1./KG2, when Do217 M-1, U5+AH Wk Nr. 40705 was shot down into the sea 20 miles S of Plymouth, Devon.

14 May 1940   He 111   7./KG 55
Ltn. Helmut Rockenhäuser (O) (58246/103), Gfr. Fritz Lüdecke (58246/155) (G) both wounded during an operational mission.

15 May 1940   He 111   8./KG 55
Ogfr. Herbert Schloms (58246/240) (W), Gfr. Willi Manegold (58246/220) (FE), Flgr. Josef Schmidt (58246/276) (G) all wounded during an operational mission in the Metz-Diedenhofen-Audun le Roman-Conflans area of France, by AA fire. Flgr. Schmidt died in hospital from his wounds on 16.8.40.

31 May 1940   He 111   9./KG 55
Uffz. Gerhard Mittelstädt (58246/348) (P), Uffz. Martin Lippert (58246/11) (FE) both injured in a crash landing on Malmsheim aerodrome, S of Karlsruhe, Germany, during a ferry flight.
Uffz. Lippert was posted 'Missing' on 29.9.40, with the rank of Feldwebel, when his He 111P G1+DT Wk Nr 2822 failed to return from a mission to attack aircraft works Nr Gloucester.

1 June 1940   He 111   8./KG 55
Fw. Ulrich Flügge (58246/212) (O) wounded during a mission to attack railway installations in the Lyon-St. Valier area, France.

2 June 1940   He 111 P-2   8./KG 55
G1+HS   Wk Nr ˙05   (P) Uffz. Horst Mahnert (582 .o/219), (O) Uffz. Hans Söhner (58246/228), (W) Uffz. Max Volkmer (58246/

233) wounded, (FE) Uffz. Willi Schubert (58246/231) wounded. (G) Gfr. Ernst-Erich-Willi Lindner (58246/268) killed. Intercepted over the Jura Mountains by four Messerschmitt Bf 109 E-3s from the 15th Fliegerkompanie of the Swiss Air Force. Shot down by Capitaine Hans Thurnheer in J-315. Crash landed Nr Ursins, Southern end of Lac de Neuchatel, Vaud, Switzerland.

2 June 1940   He111   9./KG55
Fw. Hermann Ehrentreich (58246/312), (W) Fw. Leodegar Schuderer (58246/337) and (FE,) Fw. Albert Veith (58246/342) wounded.
This is possibly the second aircraft attacked by the 15th Fliegerkompanie of the Swiss Air Force. Although there is no mention of a crash this Heinkel He 111 from 9/KG 55 was attacked. Fw. Schuderer was killed 11 May 1941, with the rank of Oberfeldwebel with 9/KG 55, when his He 111 P G1+BT Wk Nr 1619, was shot down during a mission to attack London, crashing SW of Balls Green, Nr Withyham, Sussex.

5 June 1940   He 111   7./KG 55
Uffz. Wilhelm Manger (58246/133) (BA), wounded during a mission to attack Nevers/Sermoise airfield, SE of Bourges, France. Admitted to hospital in Nagold, SW of Stuttgart, Germany where he died on 8.7.40.

5 June 1940   He 111   9./KG 55
Fw. Paul Knetsch (58246/319) (FE) wounded during a mission to attack Nevers/Sermoise airfield SE of Bourges, France.

14 June 1940   He 111   Stab/KG 55
Ofw. Karl Franz (67013/54) (P), Oblt. Wolfgang Müller (67013/31) (O), Fw. Karl Ander (67013/52) (W), Uffz. Heinz Behrens (67013/35) (FE) and Hptfw. Helmut Witt (67013/21) (G) all killed during a reconnaissance of French artillery in the Fremestroff/St. Avold area, France. Probably shot down by AA fire, the machine was seen to catch fire and crash.

7 July 1940   He 111   4./KG 55
Fw. Hans Jaffke (67014/14) (FE), reported wounded as the result of a fighter attack during a mission to attack Portland, Dorset.
Fw. Jaffke was posted 'Missing' on the Russian Front, with the rank of Oberfeldwebel, on 26.6.41.

11 July 1940   He111 H   2./KG55
(W) Ofw. Joachim Winter (67016/79) and (G) Gfr. Ernst Pestal (67016/88) wounded. Returned to Villacoublay aerodrome, France, from an attack on Portsmouth Harbour. Severely damaged by P/O J.E. Storrar from No. 145 Squadron.

11 July 1940   He111 H   2./KG 55
G1+LK   Wk Nr 2648.   (P) Ofw. Erich Slotosch (67016/65), (O) Oblt. Siegfried Schweinhagen (67016/4) and (W) Fw. Herbert,Steiner (67016/66) PoW. (FE) Ofw. Hans Schlüter (67016/59) killed, (G) Uffz. Wilhelm Müller (67016/49) died on his way to hospital. Crashed on East Beach, Selsey, S of Chichester, Sussex, during an attack on Portsmouth Harbour. Shot down by P/O Lord R.U.P. Kay-Shuttleworth and P/O E.C.J. Wakeham from No. 145 Squadron. S/Ldr. J.R.A. Peel shot down by return fire.

11 July 1940   He 111 P   2./KG 55
G1+HK   (P) Fw. Herbert Aleith (67016/
7) killed. (O) Uffz. Karl Maiereder (67016/44),
(W) Fw. Willi Ruschewitz (67016/57), (FE) Uffz.
Paul Klein (67016/39) and (G) Uffz. Alfred Reindl
(67016/54) missing. Shot down into the sea off
Selsey, Sussex, during an attack on Portsmouth
Harbour by F/Lt. R.G. Dutton of No. 145 Sqdn.

12 July 1940   He111   Stab KG55
G1+FA   (O) Oblt. Walter Kleinhanns (67013/2)
killed. (P) Fw. John-Christian Möhn (67013/106),
(W) Fw. Heinz Kalinna (67013/69), (FE) Ofw.
Fritz Knecht (67013/14) and (G) Ofw. Philipp
Mülller (67013/44) PoW. Attacked by six
Hurricane pilots from No. 43 Sqdn. S/Ldr. J.V.C.
Badger, F/Lt. T.F. Dalton- Morgan, P/O R.A. De
Mancha, P/O D.G. Gorrie, P/O H.C. Upton
(Canadian) and Sgt. C.A.H. Ayling. Crash landed
Nr. 'The Horse and Jockey' Public House, Hipley,
NW of Portsmouth Hampshire.

19 July 1940   He111 P   7./KG55
Gl+AR   (P) Uffz. Max Biskup (58246/144), (O)
Oblt. Rudi Westhaus (58246/101) and (W) Fw.
Kurt Maeder (58246/115) killed. (FE) Fw. Rudolf
Kasten (58246/114) and (G) Gfr. Arthur Meusel
(58246/135) missing. Shot down during an attack
on Southampton by F/Lt. R.G.Dutton, P/O M.A.
Newling and P/O A. Ostowicz (Polish), from No.
145 Squadron in the sea 5 miles off Shoreham-by-
Sea, Sussex.

29 July 1940   He111 P   8./KG55
Gl+CS   (P) Fw. Theodor Metzner (58246/222),
(O) Fw. Josef Markl (58246/221), (W) Uffz. Kurt
Böker (58246/241), (FE) Gfr. Ernst Ostheimer
(58246/270) and (G) Gfr. Heinz Morgenthal
(58246/223). All were eventually taken prisoner.
Crashed at Fullers Lane, SW of Newbury,
Berkshire, during a mission to attack Bristol,
possibly the Bristol Aircraft Company factory at
Filton. Hit by AA fire.

4 August 1940   He111 P   7./KG 55
G1+IR   (P) Ofw. Gerhard Geissler (58246/386)
killed. (O) Uffz. Karl Ohmann (58246/118), (W)
Uffz. Walter Weber (58246/143), (FE) Uffz.
Werner Thieme (65113/88) and (G) Uffz.
Friedrich Westphal (58246/193) missing. Failed to
return from Manchester. Presumed crashed in the
Channel.

12 August 1940   He 111P   9./KG 55
G1+HT   (P) Uffz. Herbert Schmidt
killed, Uffz. Ernst Held (58221/23) (O) killed,
Uffz. Richard Bubel (58246/310) (W) wounded,
Fw. Fritz Paulussen (58246/328) wounded.
Crashed on the return flight from a mission to
attack Bristol, Nr. Rambervillers, NE of Epinal,
France.
*Uffz. Bubel was killed on 1.11.40, when his
machine He 111P-2 Gl+JS Wk Nr 1571 was shot
down during a mission to attack London (8./KG
55).*

14 August 1940   He111 P   Stab KG 55
Gl+AA Wk Nr 2898   (P) Oblt. Bruno
Brossler (67012/3), (O) Oberst Alois Stoeckl,
Geschwaderkommodore, (67012/1) and (G)
Oberst Walther Frank (L.G.Kdo.VIII Nr. 312)
killed. (W) Fw. Heinz Grimstein (67013/86) and
(FE) Fw. Jonny Thiel (67013/6) PoW injured.
Shot down by P/O D.M. Crook and F/O J.C.

Dundas from No. 609 Squadron at the Royal
Naval Armament Depot Dean Hill, NW of
Romsey, Hampshire.

14 August 1940   He 111P   6./KG 55
Ltn. Franz Wandrey (P), Uffz. Hermann
Schoepke (67021/54) (FE), Stabsarzt Dr. Albrecht
Freiherr von Liebenstein all killed. Uffz. Fritz
Trost (67021/57) and Sanitäts Gfr. Reinhard Bink
both injured. Crashed Merzhausen, SW of
Giessen, Germany, on a domestic flight due to an
engine failure.

15 August 1940   He 111   2./KG 55
Gl+OK   (P) Ltn. Teja Zobel (67016/121)
wounded, Fw. Gustav Marx (67016/45) (O)
wounded, and Uffz. Alfons Frey (67016/109) (W)
killed. Force landed after a mission to attack
Plymouth, Devon. 70% damage. Nr Carolles, S of
Granville, France.

16 August 1940   He111P   4./KG 55
Gl+LM   (P) FW. Ernst Müller (67019/
23), (O) Hpt. Wladimir Sabler (67019/1)
Staffelkapitän, (W) Fw. Walter Magerhans
(67019/20), (FE) Uffz. Erich Schmidtke (67019/
36) and (G).Gfr. Albin Szymanowski (67019/65)
killed. Shot down by P/O G.E. Goodman of No. 1
Sqdn. Crashed at Upper Frithfold Farm, E of
Northchapel, Sussex.

16 August 1940   He111 P   6./KG55
G1+BP   (W) Fw. Paul Henze (67020/21)
and (FE) Uffz. Heinrich Wurm (67020/48)
injured.

16 August 1940   He111 P   6./KG 55
Gl+HP   (P) Oblt. Wilhelm Wieland
(67021/127) (O) Fw. Hans Langstrof (67021/49)
and (W) Uffz. Werner Appel (67021/40) PoW.
(FE) Uffz. Anton Hattendorf (67021/53) killed.
(G) Uffz. Gerhard Pulver (67021/47) died of
wounds. Shot down by S/Ldr. D.A. Pemberton
from No. 1 Squadron during an attack on
Heathrow aerodrome. Crashed at Annington
Farm, S of Bramber, Sussex.

16 August 1940   He111 P   7./KG55
Gl+FR Wk Nr 1582.   (P) Ltn. Rudolf
Theopold (58246/199), (O) Uffz. Rudolf
Hornbostel (58246/403) and (W) Gfr. Helmut
Glaser (58246/128) PoW. (FE) Uffz. Albert
Weber (58246/123) and (G) Gfr. Johannes
Moorfeld (58246/411) killed. Attacked by F/Lt.
R.F. Boyd and Blue Section of No. 602 Squadron
during an attack on Heathrow aerodrome. Crashed
at Honeysuckle Lane, High Salvington, Nr
Worthing, Sussex.

16 August 1940   He111   7./KG 55
(W) Uffz. Gerhard Dochow (58246/125), (FE)
Uffz. Heinrich Epkenhaus (58246/126) and (G)
Uffz. Wilhelm Biewald (58246/195) wounded.
Crashed Nr Le Havre, France, due engine failure
following a mission to attack Heathrow aero-
drome, Middlesex.

16 August 1940   He111 P   9./KG 55
(FE) Uffz. Paul Brzoska (58246/309) wounded.
Returned to Villacoublay aerodrome with damage
following a mission to attack Heathrow aerodrome, Middlesex.

16 August 1940   He111 P   III./KG 55
Force landed on Dreux aerodrome, due to engine
trouble after a mission to attack Heathrow
aerodrome, Middlesex. The crew were uninjured
but the machine sustained 80% damage.

23 August 1940   He111 P   3./KG55
Gl+DL   (O) Ofw. Heinrich Weber
(67017/28) wounded.(G) Gfr. Johannes Kaden
(67017/68) killed. Force landed Nr Octeville, N of
Le Havre, France, after a mission to attack
Southampton during which it was hit by AA fire.

23 August 1940   He111 H   2./KG 55
Gl+EK   (P) Oblt. Hans Mössner (67016/
3) uninjured, (O) Fw. Johann Reiter (67016/56)
uninjured, (W) Ofw. Kurt Heinze (67016/32)
wounded, (FE) Ofw. Otto Weis (67016/76)
wounded. (G) Gfr. Harald Kawlath (67016/140)
baled out over the Channel and posted missing.
Forced landed Nr. Le Havre, France, after being
damaged by fighters during a mission to attack
aircraft factories at Yeovil.

25 August 1940   He111 P   9./KG55
Gl+CT   (P) Uffz. Alois Schmaderer
(58246/398) PoW, (O) Ltn. Gustav Jerusel
(58246/306), (W) Gfr. Walter Klesatschek
(58246/397), (FE) Fw. Paul Neidel (58246/326)
and Flgr. Hans Alt, war correspondent, killed.
Shot down into the sea 1 mile off Hastings, Sussex,
during a mission to attack Bristol by F/Lt. J.G.
Sanders from No. 615 Squadron

26 August 1940   He111 P   StabI./KG 55
Gl+BB   (P) Oblt. Ignaz Krenn (67014/
31) uninjured, (O) Uffz. Helmuth Morrack
(67014/35) slightly wounded, (W) Uffz. Hans
Degen (67016/89) uninjured, (FE,) Uffz. Willi
Schneiders (67014/13) seriously wounded and (G)
Fw. Alois Schreek (67014/21) slightly wounded.
All PoWs. Attacked by S/Ldr. J.V.C. Badger and
Sgt. H.J.L. Hallowes of No. 43 Squadron. Also
No. 602 Squadron S/Ldr. A.V.R. Johnstone.
Crashed at Court Wick Farm, Wick. N of
Littlehampton, Sussex, during an attack on
Portsmouth Harbour.

26 August 1940   He111   2./KG55
Returned damaged from Portsmouth Harbour and
force landed on Dreux Aerodrome. (G) Gfr.
Günther Weidner (67016/93) wounded.

26 August 1940   He111 P   3./KG55
Gl+GL Wk Nr 5370   Returned damaged
from Portsmouth Harbour and force landed Nr. Le
Havre. (G) Gfr. Otto Tjaden (67017/80)
wounded.

26 August 1940   He111   4./KG55
Gl+AM   Returned from Portsmouth
Harbour and landed at Chartres aerodrome. (O)
Oblt. Joachim Herrfurth (67019/97) wounded.

26 August 1940   He111 P   4./KG55
Gl+DM Wk Nr 2124   (P) Ltn. Albert Metzger
(67019/103) PoW, slightly wounded. (O) Uffz.
Rolf Schandner (67019/22), (W) Uffz. Rudi Paas
(67019/30), (FE) Fw. Julius Urhahn (67019/37)
and (G) Flgr. Rudolf Fessel (67019/102) killed.
Shot down by Sgt. B.E.P. Whall from No. 602
Squadron during an attack on Portsmouth
Harbour. Crashed at Bracklesham, East Wittering,
Sussex.

26 August 1940   He111   4./KG55
Gl+GM Wk Nr 2165   (P) Ltn. Klaus Walter
(67019/127) PoW, (O) Ofw. Otto Henneeke
(670191/10) killed when he baled out too low,
(W) Uffz. Oskar Schufft (67019/120), (FE) Uffz.
Fritz Marner (67019/118) and (G) Flgr. Josef
Wimmer (67019/123) PoWs. Shot down by P/O
H.L. North of No. 43 Squadron during an attack
on Portsmouth Harbour and crashed at Westbrook
Farm, E of Waterlooville, Hampshire.

26 August 1940   He111 P   5./KG55
Gl+GN   (P) Fw. Karl Brüning (67020/
28) uninjured, (O) Oblt. Fritz von dem Hagen,
(W) Uffz. Konrad Steiger (67020/35) wounded,
(FE) Uffz. Willi Lösch (67020/62) wounded and
(G) Gfr. Gustav Stratmann (67020/81) wounded.
Attacked by P/O E.W. Aries from No. 602
Squadron and crashed in the Channel after a
mission to attack Portsmouth Harbour. The crew
were all rescued by a Seenotdienst launch.

29 August 1940   He 111   7./KG55
Gl+BR Wk Nr 2692   (P) Ltn. Heinz Nützel
(58246/197), (O) Ofw. Heinz Scheithauer
(67013/37), (W) Ogfr. Erich Schreiber (58246/
412), (FE) Fw. Karl Brohr (65113/95) and (G)
Gfr. Helmut Bretthauer (58246/407) killed.
Crashed on take off for an attack on Liverpool, at
Villacoublay aerodrome.

29 August 1940   He 111   III./KG 55
Wk Nr 2858   Force landed Nr Sens, W of
Troyes, due to fuel exhaustion after a mission.
Crew uninjured. The machine 30% damaged.

30 August 1940   He111 P   5./KG55
(P) Uffz. Ewald Berdelmann (6.Kp.Sch. F.A.R.52
Nr.75), (O) Fw. Walter Krause
(3.Kp.Fl.Erg.Batl.31 Nr.72), (W) Uffz. Kurt
Jeschonneck (67019/33) and (G) Flgr. Karl Weis
(4.F.A.R.33 Nr.398) all killed. Involved in a mid-
air collision during a formation training flight.
Crashed Nr Chartres, SW of Paris, France.

30 August 1940   He111 P   6./KG55
(P) Uffz. Horst Fink (Flzg.F.Sch.B Schoena Nr.6
(Schüko)), (BA) Gfr. Artur Hickmann
(Fl.H.Kdtr.Schoeneberg Nr.182), (W) Uffz. Adolf
Lemsky (F.A.R.21 Nr.546) and (G) Flgr. Hugo
Bräucker (67021/118) all killed. Involved in a
mid-air collision during a formation training flight.
Crashed Nr Chartres, SW of Paris, France.

30 August 1940   He111 P   8./KG 55
Gl+ES Wk Nr 2812   (P) Oblt. Hans-
Günther Nedden (58246/296), (O) Ltn. Heinz-
Martin Wronsky (53577/156), (W) Uffz. Ewald
Buchtzik (58246/244), (FE) Gfr. Horst Rosenberg
(58246/226) and (G) Gfr. Robert Dinter (58246/
260) all injured. Force landed W of Sens, France,
with a damaged starboard engine and the port
engine overheating. Damage caused by AA fire
during a mission to attack Liverpool.

30 August 1940   He111 P-2   8./KG 55
Gl+KS Wk Nr 1629   (P) Uffz. Alfred Müller
(58246/295), (O) Fw. Albert König (58246/253),
(W) Ogfr. Ludwig Groh (58246/300), (FE) Gfr.
Heinrich Friedriszik (58246/261) and (G) Ogfr.
Arno Raths (58246/299). All killed. Involved in a
collision with an He 111 P-2 Wk Nr 1703, from
the Erganzungsstaffel KG 55. Crashed Nr
Neauphle, W of Versailles, Paris.

30 August 1940   He 111 Ergst./KG 55
Ogfr. Karl Martin (67019/56) and Gfr. Johann
Dunker (67019/87) killed. Crashed Chartres
Aerodrome, SW of Paris, France.

6 September 1940   He111 P-2   6./KG 55
Gl+CP Wk Nr 1532   (P) Ltn. Hilmar
Seeliger (67021/119) killed. Crashed on outward
bound flight to Liverpool at Lisieux, E of Caen,
France. Reported to have been hit by 'friendly'
Flak.

7 September 1940   He 111 P-2   StabIII./
KG 55 Wk Nr 1731   (O) Oblt. Wolfgang
Witte (67013/118) baled out and was seriously
injured. Crashed on return flight from London due
to engine failure, 10 km S of L'Aigle, W of Dreux,
France.
Oblt. Witte was again seriously injured on 2
February 1945 when he crashed during a training
flight in a Bf 109 G-6. He was then Staffelkapän of
1.(J)/KG55 with the rank of Hauptmann. He died
22 February 1945.

7 September 1940   He111   8./KG 55
Gl+DS   (P) Ofw. Bernhard Hickel (58246/238)
and his crew baled out uninjured. Crashed due to
engine failure after a mission to attack London at
Breteuil, NE of Beauvais, France.

8 September 1940   He 111 P-2   9./KG55
Wk Nr 3353   Crashed on landing at
Villacoublay Aerodrome, S of Paris, France, due to
damage from A.A. fire after a mission to attack
London. Sustained 50% damage. Two crew
members were wounded, (P) Fw. Eduard Merz
(58246/389) and (G) Ltn. Richard Richter
(65183/2).

11 September 1940   He111 P   Stab KG/55
Gl+BA Wk Nr 2683   (P) Uffz. Walter Lange
(67013/152), (O) Fw. Kurt Eckert (67013/162),
(W) Ogfr. Artur Windmann (67013/163) and War
Correspondent Fw Heinz Holzapfel (199-
Filmst.Ausb.Bw. 133-Chef.Ausb.L.Haupt.) killed.
(FE) Gfr. Franz Koller (67013/100) injured.
Crashed Nr Villacoublay aerodrome on return
from London.

13 September 1940   He111 P-2   Stab III./
KG55   Gl+AD Wk Nr 2910   (P) Fw. Kurt
Neubacher (58246/224), (O) Ltn. Helmut
Rockenhäuser (58246/103), (W) Uffz. August
Preuss (58246/17), (FE) Fw. Georg Link (62671/
20) and (G) Ofw. Andreas Braunegger (58246/
258) all killed. Crashed Nr Etretat, NE of Le
Havre, after a mission to London.

14 September 1940   He111 P   Stab KG55
Gl+HA Wk Nr 5357   (P) Ltn. Hans-Friedrich
Parey (Fl.Fhr.Sch.Regensburg Nr.106), (O) Ltn.
Friedrich Schlink (67013/175), (W) Gfr. Otto
Wanger (67013/126) and (G) Ogfr. Wilhelm
Petersen (67013/58) killed. (FE) Fw. Josef Geiger
spent 3 days in a dinghy before being rescued by
the Seenotdienst. Shot down by F/O J.W. Villa
and Sgt. J. White of No. 72 Squadron into the sea
off Eastbourne, Sussex. Target London.

15 September 1940   He111 P-2   8./KG55
Gl+GS Wk Nr 2815   (FE) Uffz. Paul Schüll
(58246/232) killed over the target and (G) Gfr.
Paul Zornemann (58246/235) wounded in combat
with Spitfires from No. 152 Squadron. Returned

to Villacoublay aerodrome after a mission to attack
Portland, Dorset.

15 September 1940   He 111 P-2   9./KG55
Gl+AT Wk Nr 1586   (P) Uffz. Heinz Rothen,
PoW. (W) Uffz. Andreas Janson (58246/349),
(FE) Uffz. Fritz Keil (58246/347) and (G) Ogfr.
Rudolf Conrad (58246/514) killed. Crashed in the
Channel during a mission to attack Portland,
Dorset, in combat with Spitfires from No. 152
Squadron.

19 September 1940   He111 P-2   3./KG55
Gl+GL Wk Nr 2146   (P) Uffz. Willi Goliath
(67017/67), (O) Fw. Theodor Alpers (67017/10)
and (FE) Uffz. Hans Pohl (67017/52) killed. (W)
Uffz. Walter Gerss (67017/65) baled out badly
injured. Shot down by AA fire. Crashed Nr Great
Hallingbury, Essex. Target London.

25 September 1940   The various Gruppen
of KG55 put up 58 He111s to attack the Bristol
aero engine works at Filton, N of Bristol. They
were loaded with approximately 100 tons of high
explosive and 24 tons of oil bombs. The escort was
provided by Bf 110s from ZG 26. As the result of
the damage inflicted on the works production was
curtailed for many weeks. More than 250 people
were killed or injured in the attack.

25 September 1940   He111 H   1./KG55
Gl+BH Wk Nr 6305   (P) Fw. Fritz Jürges
(67015/26) PoW, (O) Hpt. Karl Köthke (67015/
3) PoW, (W) Gfr. Rudolf Weisbach (67015/113)
PoW, (G) Gfr. Josef Altrichter (67015/79)
captured badly wounded and died the same day.
(G) Flgr. Otto Müller (67015/103) PoW.
Attacked by Spitfires flown by P/O J. Curchin and
F/O T. Nowierski from No. 609 Squadron and a
Hurricane flown by P/O J.S. Wigglesworth from
No. 238 Squadron. Crashed at Westland Farm,
Ballard Down, Swanage, Dorset.

25 September 1940   He111 P   5./KG55
Gl+DN Wk Nr 2126   (P) Oblt. Gottfried
Weigel (67020/4), (O) Ofw. Alfred Narres
(67020/12), (W) Fw. Georg Engel (II) (67020/
37), (FE) Uffz. Karl Gerdsmeier (67020/50) and
(G) Gfr. Karl Geib (67020/84), all PoWs.
Abandoned by the crew after being hit by A.A. fire
from 237th Battery, 76th Heavy Anti-Aircraft
Regiment, Royal Artillery, sited at Portbury.
Crashed on Racecourse Farm, Failand, W of
Bristol.

25 September 1940   He111 P   6./KG55
Gl+AP Wk Nr 1579   (O) Oblt. Helmut
Kindor (67021/131) and (G) Uffz. Erich Turek
(65120/55) wounded. Crash landed 50% damaged
Nr Caen, France, having been damaged by fighter
attacks.
Kindor, with the rank of Hauptmann, was injured
on 20 December 1943 serving with 6/NJG 6 when
his Bf110 G-4 was shot down by an intruder.

25 September 1940   He111 P   6./KG55
Gl+EP Wk Nr 1525   (P) Hpt. Hellmuth
Brandt (65119/64) PoW. (O) Ofw. Günter
Wittkamp (67021/21), (W) Ofw. Rudolf
Kirchhoff (67021/14), (FE) Uffz. Hans-Fritz
Mertz (67021/41) and (G) Gfr. Rudolf Beck
(67021/116) all killed. Shot down in combat with
Spitfires flown by P/O D.W. Williams, F/O I.N.
Bayles and Sgt. K.C. Holland from No. 152

Squadron, with P/O J.R. Urwin-Mann and Sgt. R. Little from No. 238 Squadron flying Huricanes. Crashed at Church Farm, Nr. Woolverton, NE of Frome, Somerset.
Sergeant K.C. Holland crashed in his Spitfire (N3173) Nr Church Farm, Woolverton, and was killed. Possibly shot down by return fire, but it also seems possible that he crashed while performing a low altitude roll over the site of the crash.

25 September 1940   He111 P   7./KG55
Gl+LR Wk Nr 2803   (W) Uffz. Kurt Schraps (58246/141) baled out and taken prisoner. (P) Oblt. Hans Bröcker (58246/5) Staffelkapitän, (O) Oblt. Heinz-Harry Scholz (58246/204), (FE) Uffz. Günter Weidner (58246/151) and (G) Uffz. Josef Hanft (58246/194) all killed. Damaged by P/O E.S. Marrs in a Spitfire from No. 152 Squadron. Eventually shot down by P/O N. le C. Agazarian and P/O R.F.G. Miller from No. 609 Squadron. Also attacked by a by P/O J.R. Urwin-Mann in a Hurriacne from No. 238 Squadron. Crashed into a house called Underwood, on the corner of Westminster/Pinewood Road, Branksome, Dorset.

25 September 1940   He111   8./KG55
(P) Uffz. Johann Boos (58240/242) wounded. Returned to its base at Villacoublay.
Boos, with the rank of Oberfeldwebel, was awarded the Ritterkreuz on 9 October 1943 serving with 9./KG 55. Reported to have flown the last aircraft out of beleaguered Stalingrad, Russia.

26 September 1940   He111   Stab I./KG55
(P) Fw. Heinz Jelen (67015/57) wounded. Returned to Dreux aerodrome after a mission to attack Southampton

26 September 1940   He111 H   2./KG55
Gl+GK Wk Nr 5314   (P) Oblt. Hans-Hermann Graf von Schweinitz (67016/110), (O) Uffz. Heinrich Widmann (67016/78), (W) Uffz. Werner Schob (67016/91), (FE) Gfr. Erich Wastian (67016/90) and (G) Gfr. Richard Helfer (67016/118) all missing. Reported to have been involved in combat with Hurricanes from No. 229 Squadron and crashed into the sea 10 km S of the Isle of Wight, during a mission to attack Southampton.

26 September 1940   He111 P   3./KG55
Gl+BL Wk Nr 3098   (P) Oblt. Adalbert Karbe (67017/3) Staffelkapitän, (O) Ofw. Friedrich Wilser (67017/29) both wounded. Force landed on Dreux aerodrome, after a mission to attack Southampton, Hampshire, where it was attacked by fighters. Sustained 40% damage.
Karbe was awarded the Ritterkreuz on 12 November 1941 and killed on 30 July 1942 when shot down near Weymouth, Dorset.

29 September 1940   He111 P   9./KG55
Gl+BT Wk Nr 2820   (P) Uffz. Adolf Fernberg (58246/501), (O) Fw. Karl Blessing (58246/395), (W) Uffz. Gerhard Hemmerle (58246/317), (FE,) Ogfr. Friedrich Nuscher (58246/351) and (G) Gfr. Heinz Tasche (58246/505) all injured. Force landed Nr St. Lo, W of Caen. Reported to have been hit by AA fire during a mission to attack an aircraft factory Nr Gloucester.

29 September 1940   He 111 P   9./KG55
Gl+DT Wk Nr 2822   (P) Oblt. Hans Köhler (58246/303) missing, (O) Fw. Horst Birkholz (58246/209) killed, (W) Uffz. Rudolf Firchau (58246/314) killed, (FE) Fw. Martin Lippert (58246/11) missing, (G) Gfr. Franz Günther (58246/354) killed. Shot down by No. 79 Squadron. Crashed into the sea in St. George's Channel, W of Wales, during a mission to attack an aircraft factory Nr Gloucester.

30 September 1940   He111 P-2   8./KG55
Gl+CM Wk Nr 2643   (P) Gfr. Erich Rudeck (67019/121) missing, (O) Ofw. Helmut Güttler (67019/88) killed, (W) Gfr. Karl Bauer (67019/64) missing, (FE) Gfr. Fritz Strauss (67019/81) missing and (G) Gfr. Willi Schocke (65113/59) killed. Involved in combat with Hurricanes from Nos. 238 and 504 Squadrons during an attack on Westland's, Yeovil, and shot down into the sea off Portland, Dorset.

30 September 1940   He111   5./KG55
Gl+LN   (O) Fw. Helmut Zimmermann (67020/104) killed. Reported to have been attacked by fighters on the Westland mission and returned to Chartres aerodrome.

30 September 1940   He111   1./KG55
Gl+IH   (FE) Fw. Wilhelm Steidel (67015/41) wounded. Returned to Dreux aerodrome after a mission to attack Yeovil, Somerset.

30 September 1940   He111   2./KG55
(G) Gfr. Paul Thieme (67016/68) wounded. Returned to Dreux aerodrome after a mission to attack Yeovil, Somerset.

30 September 1940   He111   3./KG 55
(W) Ofw. Rudolf Arend (67017/11) wounded. Returned to Dreux aerodrome after a mission to attack Yeovil, Somerset.

30 September 1940   He111 P-2   3./KG55
Gl+AL Wk Nr 1616   (P) Oblt. Hans Mössner (67016/3), (O) Uffz. Johann Reiter (67016/56), (W) Uffz. Johannes Trenkmann (67016/69), (FE) Gfr. Thümel and (G) Flgr. Anton Geist all safe. Ditched in the Channel.

30 September 1940   He111 P-2   4./KG 55
Gl+AM Wk Nr 1545   (P) Uffz. Emil Eggert (67019/129), (O) Uffz. Rudolf Kübler (67019/100), (W) Ogfr. Willy Geyer (67019/101), (FE) Gfr. Willy Rösel (60026/59) and (G) Gfr. Willi Biedermann (67019/116) all killed. Shot down by fighters into the Channel after a mission to attack Yeovil, Somerset.

30 September 1940   He111 P-2
Geschwaderstab KG55   Gl+JA Wk Nr 2836
(P) Uffz. Robert Barabas (67013/98) killed. (O) Maj. Ernst Kühl (67012/2) injured, (W) Uffz. Rudolf Steglich uninjured, (FE) Gfr. Sebastian Feichtmair (67013/137) injured and (G) Gfr. Rolf-Siegfried Becker (67013/139) injured. The survivors were rescued by a Seenotdienst aircraft, and were admitted to hospital in Cherbourg, France. Shot down by P/O N. le C. Agazarian from No. 609 Squadron and ditched in the Channel following a mission to Yeovil, Somerset.
Dr. Ernst Kühl was Geschwaderkommodore 27.8.1942 - 7.8.1943. Awarded the Ritterkreuz 17.10.1942 Eichenlaub 18.12.1943. Died 1972.

8 October 1940   He 111 P-2   6./KG55
Gl+AP Wk Nr 1619   (P) Ofw. Heinrich Struckmeier (71032/109) wounded. Hit by A.A. fire during a mission to Eastleigh.

8 October 1940   He 111 P-2   8./KG55
Gl+BS Wk Nr 2809   (O) Uffz. Herbert Heinzl (58246/293) and (G) Uffz. Josef Bogner (58246/264) wounded. Returned to Villacoublay aerodrome after an attack on Thorney Island aerodrome.

8 October 1940   He111 P-2   8./KG55
Gl+MS Wk Nr 1715   (P) Fw. Ernst Ens (58246/237), (O) Ltn. Ulrich Flügge (58246/212), (W) Uffz. Johann Ehrensberger (58246/211), (FE) Uffz. Ernst Herber (58246/214) and (G) Gfr. Hans Pawlik (58246/271) killed. Shot down by ground fire and exploded on impact at Stansted Park, W of Stoughton, Sussex. Target Thorney Island aerodrome.

8 October 1940   He 111   9./KG 55
Gfr. Herbert von dem Heyden (58246/392) (G) wounded. Returned after a mission to attack Thorney Island aerodrome, Sussex.

15 October 1940   He 111 P-2   4./KG55
Gl+DM Wk Nr 1542   (P) Ltn. Wolfgang Hansen (67019/7) and (O) Uffz. Horst Reinbold (67019/61) wounded. Force landed Nr Cherbourg, due to engine damage during the attack on Yeovil.

20 October 1940   He 111   8./KG 55
Gl+HS   (P) Ofw. Bernhard Hickel (58246/238) and his crew were uninjured. On landing at Villacoublay aerodrome, S of Paris, France after an operational mission, the machine was destroyed due to the ignition of an incendiary bomb that had 'hung-up'. Target not recorded.

24 October 1940   He 111P-4 II Stab/KG 55 Wk Nr 3100   Ofw. Heinz Jesuiter (67017/20) (P) and Fw. Ernst Gass (67018/11) (FE) both killed. Machine crashed during a routine domestic flight when it ran into bad weather on its return from Berlin/Teltow aerodrome. Nr Halberstadt, SW of Magdeburg, Germany.

24 October 1940   He 111H-2 Ergst/KG 55 Wk Nr 5330   Oblt. Erich Wamser (53577/850) (P), Gfr. Karl Krecht (53577/838) (BA), Uffz. Paul Materna (53577/840) (W), Gfr. Rudolf Bach (67020/93) (FE) and Flgr. Alfred Hentschel (53577/808) (G) all killed. Crashed in flames during a local training flight, Nr Kamenz, NE of Dresden, Germany. Cause unknown.

26 October 1940   He 111 P-2
Geschwaderstab KG55   Gl+EA Wk Nr 2653
(P) Ltn. Franz Oberhofer (67013/141), (O) Oblt. Bodo Eitner (67013/170), (W) Gfr. Michael Schweikert (67013/172), (FE) Uffz. Kurt Kümmel (67013/19), and (G) Uffz. Herbert Kemlitz (67013/160) all killed. Crashed 1 km N of Versailles, after a mission to attack London.

26 October 1940   He111 P-2   II./KG55
Wk Nr 3354   Crashed on landing at Cormeilles-en-Vexin aerodrome, after a mission to London. There were no crew casualties, but the machine sustained 25% damage.

26 October 1940   He111 P-2
Geschwaderstab KG55   Wk Nr 2666
Crashed on landing at Villacoublay and struck a 'Splitterwall' after a mission to London. Aircraft written off. No crew casualties.

1 November 1940   He 111 P-2 8./KG55
Gl+JS Wk Nr 1571   (P) Ltn. Hans-Adalbert Tüffers (58246/510) PoW, (Ò) Uffz. Josef Haverstreng (55336/44) PoW, (W) Uffz. Richard Bubel (58246/310) and (FE) Uffz. Josef Juvan (65183/13) killed. Hit by AA fire during a sortie to the Victoria Docks, London, and crashed at Matlock Gardens, Hornchurch, Essex.

13 November 1940   He111 P-4 5./KG55
Gl+GN Wk Nr 2994   (G) Fw. Karl Hauber (67020/51) killed. Attacked by fighters during a sortie to Bristol. Returned to Chartres aerodrome.

19 November 1940   He111 P-4 2./KG55
Gl+LK Wk Nr 2877   (P) Oblt. Hans Klawe (67016/111) found dead in the aircraft, (O) Fw. Wilhelm Gutekunst (67016/30) baled out PoW, (W) Uffz. Rudolf Zeitz (67016/89) baled out PoW, (G) Gfr. Xaver Nirschel (67016/138) found dead in the aircraft. Shot down by AA fire and crashed at Worksop Farm, Wolvey, Warwickshire.

20 November 1940   He111 P-4 3./KG55
Wk Nr 2948   (P) Oblt. Adalbert Karbe (67017/3) injured. Landed on Dreux aerodrome, 70% damage, after a sortie to Birmingham. Three other crew members also reported to have been injured.

24 November 1940   He111 H-4 5./KG55
Gl+KN Wk Nr 3092   (P) Ofw. Werner Müller (67020/30) missing, (O) Ltn. Gerhard Heiland (67020/19) missing, (W) Fw. Heinrich Gaick (67020/68) missing, (FE) Stfw. Heinrich Heidt (67020/14) killed and (War Correspondent) Sdrfhr. Emil Weihmüller missing. Hit by AA fire during a sortie to Bristol. Crashed into the sea 300 yards off Rame Head SW of Plymouth, Devon.

8 December 1940   He111 P-2 9./KG55
Gl+LT Wk Nr 3354   (P) Ltn. Walter Lehenbauer (53911/156), (O) Uffz. Heinz Herrmann (58246/390), (W) Fw. Gottfried Schreier (67020/40) and (FE) Pw. Karl Reis (67020/53) all killed. Crashed on take off at Villacoublay aerodrome. The target was to have been London.

21 December 1940   He111 P-2 7./KG55
Gl+ER Wk Nr 2133   (P) Uffz. Ernst Würthner (58246/65), (O) Gfr. Richard Tillak (58246/66), (W) Uffz. Rudolf Merker (58246/134), and (FE) Fw. Siegfried Schilbach (58246/152) all killed. Crashed on Beaumont-le-Roger aerodrome, Nr. Evreux, on the return Liverpool.

22 December 1940   He111 P-4 3./KG55
Gl+PL Wk Nr 3107   (P) Uffz. Bruno Zimmermann (67017/118) killed, (O) Fw. Walter Richter (67014/21) PoW, (W) Gfr. Adolf Waibel (67017/119) and (G) Gfr. August Wroblewski (67017/120) killed. Shot down by P/O J.G. Benson and Sgt. P. Blain in a Defiant from No. 141 Squadron. Crashed in the garden of Underwood House, SW of Etchingham, Sussex. The target was Manchester.

12 March 1941   He 111 P-4 5./KG55
Gl+GN Wk Nr 2994   (P) Stfw. Karl Brüning (67020/28) PoW, (O) Fw. Alexander Düssel (67020/32), (W) Fw. Konrad Steiger (67020/35), and (FE) Ofw. Willi Weisse (67020/22) killed. Shot down by P/O F.D. Hughes with Sgt. F. Gash. In a Defiant of No. 264 Squadron. Crashed at Denne Farm, Ockley, Surrey, during a mission to attack Liverpool/Birkenhead.

12 March 1941   He111 P-4 6./KG55
Gl+CP Wk Nr 2989   (P) Ofw. Karl Single (67021/111) PoW, (O) Hpt. Wolfgang Berlin (67016/2) Staffelkapitän PoW, (W) Fw. Xaver Diem (67021/44) PoW, (FE) Fw. Leonhard Kuznik (67021/38) killed and (G) Fw. Heinrich-Johann Ludwinski (67021/138) Killed. Shot down by Sgt. MacNair in Hurricane from No. 96 Squadron during a mission to attack Liverpool/Birkenhead and crashed at the rear of the I.C.I. Sportsground, Ball o' Ditton, Widnes, Lancashire.

13 March 1941   He111 P-2
Geschwaderstab KG55   Gl+HA Wk Nr 2859   (W) Uffz. Hermann von dem Burg wounded and (G) Fw. Herbert Brannat (67013/45) killed. Brannat is reported to have been killed over Oxford during a fighter attack. Crashed in the Channel after a mission to attack Liverpool.

13 March 1941   He111 P-2 7./KG55
Gl+MR Wk Nr 2806   (P) Oblt. Walter Hesse (58246/58) Staffelkapitän PoW (O) Fw. Gottfried Groschopf (58246/252) PoW, (W) Ofw. Bernhard Manek (58246/109) killed and (FE) Fw. Helmut Klein (67020/54) killed. Crashed at Wood Farm, NE of Bramdean, Hampshire, during a mission to Liverpool. Shot down by P/O A.J. Hodgkinson and Sgt. B.E. Dye in a Beaufighter from No. 219 Squadron.

14 March 1941   He111 P-4 6./KG55
Gl+IM Wk Nr 3095   (P) Ltn. Eitel Barth injured, (O) Uffz. Ulrich Schuster (67021/115) killed, (W) Uffz. August-Emil Grimmig (67018/34) wounded and (FE) Uffz. Martin Wallrabenstein injured. Belly landed on Cherbourg Aerodrome after a mission to Glasgow

14 March 1941   He111 P-4 6./KG55
Gl+JP Wk Nr 3096   (P) Oblt. Eckehardt Henschke (53911/103) Staffelführer, (O) Fw. Franz Härter (67019/58), (W) Fw. Heinz Krüger (53911/19) and (FE) Fw. Willi Smolinski (53911/41) all killed. Shot down by F/O K.I. Geddes and Sgt. A.C. Cannon in a Beaufighter from No. 604 Squadron during a mission to Glasgow. Crashed at Horseshoe Farm, 2 miles S of Falfield, Gloucestershire.

14 March 1941   He111 8./KG55
Gl+GS   (P) Ofw. Bernhard Hickel (58246/238) uninjured, (W) Fw. Herbert Schloms (58246/240) wounded and (FE) Fw. Fritz Drechsel (58246/279) wounded. Landed with the port wing on fire on Le Bourget aerodrome, Paris, after being attacked by a night fighter on a mission to Liverpool.

14 March 1941   He111 8./KG55
Gl+KS   (FE) Fw. Paul Brzoska (58246/309) wounded. Returned to Villacoublay aerodrome after a mission to Liverpool.

15 March 1941   He111 P-2 Stab/KG55
Gl+DA Wk Nr 2838   (P) Uffz. Klaus Bauer (67013/198), (O) Gfr. Josef Strauch (67013/200), (W) Gfr. Eduard Utikal (67013/201) and (FE) Uffz. Josef Schuhmacher (67013/199) all missing. Failed to return from a mission to London.

15 March 1941   He111 P-2 7./KG55
Gl+KR Wk Nr 2795   (P) Ltn. Wilhelm Räuchle (58246/401) missing, (O) Uffz. Wolfgang Stäps (58246/404) missing, (W) Ofw. Richard Both (58246/417) killed and (FE) Fw. Albert Waschto (58246/122) missing. Crashed in the Channel during the mission to London.

19 March 1941   He111 8./KG55
Fw. Franz Lindenkamp (58246/13) (FE) killed on the return flight from London.

2 April 1941   He111 P-2 7./KG55
Gl+IR Wk Nr 2137   (P) Uffz. Hans Wagner (58246/419) missing, (O) Oblt. Hans-Ludwig Wolff 62674/115) killed, (W) Uffz. Karl Papadi (58246/421) missing. (FE) Ofw. Wilhelm Bürkle 69011/25) missing and (G) Uffz. Robert Ehlers (58246/418) missing. Failed to return from a sea-reconnaissance mission. Shot down into the sea 2 miles S of Budleigh Salterton, Devon, by F/Lt. P. T. Parsons in a Hurricane of No. 504 Squadron.

8 April 1941   He111 P-4 1./KG55
Gl+KH Wk Nr 2976   (P) Ofw. Heinrich Schwiering (67015/112), (O) Fw. Werner Ehrlich (67015/63), (W) Fw. Wilhelm Letzgus (67015/65) and (FE) Ofw. Ernst Nottmeier (67015/59) all killed. Shot down by P/O A.J. Hodgkinson and Sgt. B.E. Dye in a Beaufighter from No. 219 Squadron during a mission to Greenock, Scotland. Crashed into the sea off Worthing, Sussex.

9 April 1941   He111 P-4 3./KG55
G1+DL Wk Nr 2962   (P) Ofw. Heinz Söllner (67017/26), (O) Hpt. Otto Bodemeyer (67014/2) Gruppenkommandeur I./KG55. (W) Fw. Hans Kaufhold (67017/42) and (FE) Fw. Herbert Link (67017/49) all PoW. Shot down by P/O R.P. Stevens DFC in a Hurricane from No. 151 Squadron during a mission to Coventry and crashed at Roe's Rest Farm, Peckleton, Leicestershire.

9 April 1941   He111 P-2 5./KG55
Gl+DN Wk Nr 1423   (P) Uffz. Alfred Müller (Sch./P.A.R.10 Nr.148) killed, (O) Gfr. Rudolf Langhans (3.(E).A.R.109 mit Nr.100) killed, (W) Gfr. Heinrich Berg (13./Lg.Nachr.Rgt.l/ Nr.702) PoW and (FE) Uffz. Gerhard Neumann (67020/113) killed. Shot down by F/Sgt. E.R. Thorn DFM and Sgt. F.J. Barker DFM in a Defiant from No. 264 Squadron during a mission to Birmingham. Crashed at Lodge Bottom, Busbridge, Surrey.

9 April 1941   He111 P-4 8./KG55
Gl+LS   (P) Ofw. Franz Vonier (58246/234) killed, (O) Oblt. Jürgen Bartens (58246/202) Staffelkapitän killed, (W) Ofw. Fritz Pons (58246/225) PoW, (FE) Fw. Hermann Kübler (58246/245) PoW. Shot down by F,/Lt. D.A.P. McMullen DFC and Bar, and Sgt. S.T. Fairweather in a Defiant from No. 151 Squadron during a mission to Coventry. Crashed in Windsor Great Park, Berkshire.

9 April 1941   He111 P-4   5./KG55
Gl+BN   Wk Nr 2960   Fw. Wilhelm
Schmeling (67020/73 (W) wounded. Fw.
Gottfried Keppler (67020/76) (FE) killed.
Returned to Chartres aerodrome after a mission to
Birmingham, 25% damaged by fighters.

11 April 1941   He111 P-4   2./KG55
Gl+NK   Wk Nr 2873   (P) Ltn. Werner
Lohmann, (O) Gfr. Walter Rappel (67021/134),
(W) Fw. Julius Tröger (67016/70) and (FE) Fw.
Fritz Ahorner (67016/6) all missing. Failed to
return from a mission to Birmingham. Probably
crashed in the Channel.

11 April 1941   He111 P-4   3./KG55
Gl+EL   Wk Nr 2946   (P) Ltn. Hans-Kaspar
Graf von Krockow (67015/9) killed, (O) Ofw.
Rudolf Maudrey (67015/46) killed, (W) Fw.
Siegfried Gebhardt (67015/77) killed, (FE) Fw.
Franz Huhmann and (G) Uffz. Christian Bauer
uninjured. Crashed into the sea off Trouville, S of
Le Havre, on the return from a mission to attack
Birmingham.

11 April 1941   He111 P-2   7./KG55
G1+LR   Wk Nr 1617   (P) Ltn. Ludwig-Gustav
Prinz Biron von Curland (582461/436), (O) Ofw.
Walter Wünsch (58246/433), (W) Fw. Hans
Hiestand (67021/971, and (FE) Gfr. Kurt Klipp
(53577/806) all missing. Failed to return from a
mission to attack Birmingham. Probably crashed in
the Channel.

11 April 1941   He111 P-2   9./KG55
Gl+IT   Wk Nr 2827   (P) Ltn. Günther Buse
(58246/524) PoW, (O) Fw. Wilhelm Kanera
(58246/530) died of injuries, (W) Willi Scheele
(58246/526) killed due to parachute failure, (FE)
Uffz. Kurt Roick (58246/331) killed due to
parachute failure, (G) Uffz. Franz Schober (58246/
545) found dead in the aircraft. Shot down by P/O
R.P. Stevens DFC Hurricane from No. 151
Squadron. Crashed Nr. Rothwell Lodge,
Kettering, Northamptonshire.

12 April 1941   He111 P-2   8./KG55
Gl+GS   Wk Nr 1401   (P) Gfr. Bruno Rode
(67016/105), (O) Uffz. Erich Rähse (58246/474),
(W) Uffz. Walter Ulbricht (67016/98) and (FE)
Gfr. Karl Berger (58246/473) all missing. Crashed
into the sea N of Cherbourg, due to engine failure
after a mission to Bristol/Avonmouth.

14 April 1941   He111 P-2   StabKG55
Gl+HA Wk Nr 1698   (P) Ltn. Werner Pröhl
(67013/16) missing, (O) Fw. August Stenull
(67013/123) killed, (W) Uffz. Fritz Drews
(67013/97) missing, (FE) Gfr. Bernhard Zeidler
(67013/171) killed and (G) Gfr. Erich Weidauer
(67013/155) killed. Failed to return from a 'special
mission'. Crashed into the sea N of Caen, France.

15 April 1941   He111 P-2   8./KG55
Gl+DS   Wk Nr 2812   (P) Fw. Fritz Költsch,
(O) Gfr. Hubert Häffner (67017/97), PoW, (W)
Uffz. Herbert Czaplinski (58246/478) PoW and
(FE) Ogfr. Heinrich Schmidt (58246/475) PoW.
Aircraft returned to base at Villacoublay, France,
minus three of its crew who baled out when hit by
AA fire during a mission to Belfast. Crash landed
with 35% damage.

16 April 1941   He111 P-2   8./KG55
Gl+ES   Wk Nr 2857   (P) Oblt. Günther von
Seidlitz (67014/4) killed (O) Fw. Franz Hümmer
(58246/216) killed, (W) Uffz. Herbert Sauer
(58246/227), PoW and (FE) Uffz. Horst
Rosenberg (58246/226) PoW. Shot down by S/
Ldr. J. Cunningham and Sgt. C.F. Rawnsley in a
Beaufighter from No. 604 Squadron during a
mission to Belfast. Crashed into 10 & 12 Padwell
Road, Southampton, Hampshire.

16 April 1941   He111 P-4   Stab II./
KG55   Gl+AC   Wk Nr 3094   (P) Ofw.
Walter Fraedrich (67020/27), (O) Oblt. Erich
Pawlak (67018/5) Ia Staff Operations Officer, (W)
Ofw. Adolf Burschik (67020/34) and (FE) Ofw.
Hans Volg (67020/45) all missing. Shot down by
F/Lt. Gomm & P/O Curnow in a Beaufighter
from No. 604 Squadron. Crashed into the sea off
Portland Bill, Dorset during a mission to Belfast.

17 April 1941   He 111 P-4   6./KG55
Gl+IP   Wk Nr 1734   (P) Ogfr. Gerhard
Reisert (67021/148), (O) Uffz. Franz Maiwald
(67021/147), (W) Gfr. Fritz Siegert (67021/149),
and (FE) Gfr. Joseph Dietrich (67021/150) all
killed. Crashed on landing after a mission to
London, at Chartres aerodrome.

22 April 1941   He111 P-4   3./KG55
Gl+FL   Wk Nr 2987   (P) Ltn. Hans Conrady
(67017/125), (O) Ofw. Herbert Findeisen
(67021/113), (W) Gfr. Rudolf Richter (67017/
123) and (FE) Uffz. Waldemar Schmidt (67017/
126) all missing. Failed to return from a mission to
Plymouth/Devonport, Devon. Reported to have
crashed in the Channel.

22 April 1941   He111 P-4   I./KG55
Wk Nr 1551   Crashed and burst into flames
Nr Evreux, after being abandoned by its crew
following a mission to Plymouth/Devonport,
Devon. No crew casualties were reported.

23 April 1941   He111 P-4   II./KG55
Wk Nr 2983   Crash landed on Chartres
aerodrome, following a mission to attack
Plymouth/Devonport, Devon. Sustained 20%
damage. No crew casualties were reported.

26 April 1941   He111   10./KG55
Gl+BU   Returned to Dijon/Longvic aerodrome,
France. (FE) Ofw. Willi Schultze killed during an
attacked by a night fighter over Bristol.

5 May 1941   He111 P-4   4./KG55
Gl+GM   Wk Nr 2942   (P) Gfr. Karl Decker
(2.F.A.R.72 Nr. 106), (O) Gfr. Gerhard Christoph
(8.M.G.J.R.28 Friedek Nr. 56), (W) Gfr. Heinz
Reichert (Lw.Baukp.mot.2 Nr. 553) and (FE) Gfr.
Franz Perzinger (3.F.A.R.14 Klagenfurt Nr. 307)
all killed. Crashed near La Ferte Vidame, NW of
Chartres, France, on outbound flight to Glasgow.

8 May 1941   He111 P-4   3./KG55
Gl+LL   Wk Nr 2874   (P) Ltn. Heinz
Dunkerbeck (67017/121) PoW, (O) Fw. Fritz
Kitzing (67017/137), (W) Uffz. Joachim
Salm (67017/100) killed and (FE) Uffz. Alfred
Gentzsch (67017/129) killed. Shot down by P/O
D. Toone and F/O R.L. Lamb in a Defiant from
No. 256 Squadron. Crashed in marshes 1 mile NE
of Bagillt Police Station, NW of Flint, Flintshire,
during an attack on Liverpool.

8 May 1941   He111 P-4   1./KG55
Gl+GH   Wk Nr 1724   (P) Ltn. Günther
Becker (53415/8), (O) Uffz. Emil Vieser (67017/
106), (W) Uffz. Edgar Faulhaber (67015/105) and
(FE) Ofw. Georg Lunz (53415/12) all missing.
Failed to return from an attack on Liverpool.

8 May 1941   He111 P-4   3./KG55
Gl+KL   Wk Nr 2951   (P) Ltn. Alexander
Wolff (67017/93) drowned, (O) Uffz. Willibald
Amann (67017/103) drowned, (W) Uffz. Eduard
Ante (67017/101) missing, (FE) Fw. Paul Tibusch
(53619/42) drowned and Flgr. Cornell
Mildenberger (Lw.K.B.Kp.5) drowned. Shot down
by Sgt. Wright and Sgt. Vaughan in a Beaufighter
from No. 604 Squadron. Crashed into the sea off
Portland, Dorset, during a mission to Liverpool.

8 May 1941   He111 P-4   6./KG55
Gl+HP Wk Nr 2908   (P) Fw. Walter
Hottenrott (67021/139), (O) Uffz. Paul Götze
(67021/108), (W) Uffz. Karl Gerstle (3/
1.St.Erg.K.Gr.3) and (FE) Ofw. Hermann Reese
(67021/33) all killed. Shot down by F/Lt. D.R.
West and Sgt. Adams in a Defiant from No. 256
Squadron. Crashed at Llwyn Knottia Farm,
Queen's Park, Wrexham, Denbighshire, during a
mission to Liverpool.

8 May 1941   He111 P-2   III./KG55
Wk Nr 1709   Crash landed on Villacoublay
aerodrome, and sustained 20% damage after being
attacked by a night fighter during a mission to
Liverpool.

8 May 1941   He111 P-4   1./KG55
G1+LH   Wk Nr 2971   (P) Oblt. Adolf
Knöringer (67015/4) Adjutant, (O) Ofw. Alois
Kloos (67015/28), (W) Uffz. Ludwig Rathsam
(58246/425) and (FE) Ofw. Karl Kohlhepp
(67015/21) all PoW. Shot down by F/Lt. E.C.
Deanesly and Sgt. W. Scott in a Defiant from No.
256 Squadron during a mission to Liverpool.
Crashed Nr Hazel Grove, SE of Stockport,
Cheshire.

9 May 1941   He111 P-4   6./KG55
Gl+FP   Wk Nr 3000   (P) Fw. Gerhard Ender
(67021/140) killed, (O) Fw. Heinrich Müller
(12.(M.G.)I.R.485 Nr. 14) PoW, (W) Uffz. Bruno
Schakat (51825/86) killed and (FE) FW. Georg
Schopf (67021/48) PoW. Shot down by F/Lt.
R.M. Trousdale and Sgt. F.J.W. Chumm in a
Defiant from No. 255 Squadron. Crashed at Long
Riston, NE of Beverley, Yorkshire, during a
mission to Sheffield.

10 May 1941   He111 P-4   I./KG55
Wk Nr 2936   Force landed in the Channel
after a mission to London. No crew casualties were
reported.

10 May 1941   He111 H-8   9./KG55
Wk Nr 3971   (P) Oblt. Johannes Speck von
Sternberg (58246/388) Staffelkapitän, killed, (O)
Fw. Fritz Muhn (58246/405) killed, (W) Gefr.
Rudolf Budde (58246/546) PoW and (FE) Fw.
Siegfried Rühle (58246/333) killed. Shot down
during a mission to Birmingham and crashed at
Fulford Hall Farm, Earlswood, S of Birmingham.

11 May 1941   He111 P-2   7./KG55
Gl+AR   Wk Nr 1469   (P) Fw. Heinz Behr
(58246/146), (O) Uffz. Ruppert Leisser (58246/
137), (W) Uffz. Arthur Knispel (58246/147), (FE)
Gfr. Helmut Kotlorz (58246/507) and (G) Gfr.
Herbert Horanek (58246/105) all missing. Failed
to return from a mission to London. Believed to
have crashed in the North Sea.

11 May 1941   He111 P-2   7./KG55
Gl+KR   Wk Nr 1409   (P) Fw. Richard
Blümich (58246/112) killed, (O) Fw. Edmund
Mehlber (58246/116) killed, (W) Uffz. Wilhelm
Ahrens (58246/431) killed, (FE) Gfr. Herbert von
dem Heyden (58246/392) missing and (G) Gfr.
Josef Moritz (58246/68) missing. Failed to return
from a mission to London. Believed to have
crashed in the North Sea.

11 May 1941   He111 P-2   9./KG55
Gl+BT   Wk Nr 1619   (P) Stfw. Adolf Schied
(58246/334) killed, (O) Ltn. Martin Reiser
(58246/513) PoW, (W) Ofw. Leodegar Schuderer
(58246/337) killed and (FE) Ofw. Lorenz Huber
(58246/315) killed. Shot down by F/Lt. D.A.P.
McMullen DFC and Sgt. S.J. Fairweather DFM in
a Defiant from No. 151 Squadron. Crashed at
Balls Green, Sussex, during a mission to London.

11 May 1941   He111 P-4   2./KG55
Gl+CK   Wk Nr 2958   (W) Uffz. Heinz
Bornstedt (67013/93) wounded. (FE) Uffz.
Walter Hofmann (67021/104) wounded. Crash
landed on Chartres aerodrome and written off,
after a mission to attack London.

11 May 1941   He 111 P-4   2./KG55
Gl+HK   Wk Nr 2974   (P) Oblt. Bruno
Lumma (53577/813) killed, (O) Ofw. Georg
Mannier (12 - 2. - I.R. Nr. 464) missing, (W)
Uffz. Gerhard Arndt (58246/208) missing, (FE)
Uffz. Reinhold Kretschmann (65112/83) killed
and War Correspondent Uffz. Heinrich Martin
(Lw.Kb.Kp. 5) missing. Failed to return from a
mission to London

11 May 1941   He111   4./KG55
Gl+DM   (O) Uffz. Werner Gramkow
(67019/139) was wounded by AA fire. Returned to
Chartres aerodrome after a mission to Tangmere
aerodrome, Sussex.

12 May 1941   He111 P-2   8./KG55
Gl+ES   Wk Nr 2858   (P) Fw. Willy Wimmer
(58246/466) killed, (O) Oblt. Horst Gündel
(58246/522) Staffelkapitän killed, (W) Fw.
Heinrich Neuber (58246/465) killed, (FE) Uffz.
Karl Scheuringer (58246/60) PoW and (G) Gfr.
Karl Röhl (58246/467) PoW. Crashed into the sea
between Wych Channel and Middle Channel,
Poole Harbour, Dorset.

17 May 1941   He111 P-2   7./KG55
Gl+GR   Wk Nr 2801   (P) Ltn. Helmut Pichler
(58246/198), (O) Fw. Berthold Abraham (58246/
140), (W) Fw. Lorenz Stöger (67019/130) and
(FE) Ofw. Kurt Seefeld (58246/119) all killed.
Shot down by P/O A.J. Hodgkinson DFC and Sgt.
B.E. Dye in a Beaufighter from No. 219 Squadron.
Crashed on the Downs, N of Worthing. Sussex,
during a mission to Birmingham.

27 May 1941   He111 H-8   4./KG55
Gl+AM   Wk Nr 3867   (P) Fw. Lorenz Kempel
(67019/136), (O) Uffz. Kurt Nuglan (67020/122),
(W) Fw. Otto Stadel (67019/69), (FE) Fw. Martin
Göbel (Sch./F.A.R.24 Nr. 480) and (G) Gfr. Josef
Wiederer (4./F.A.R.53 Nr. 359) all killed. Shot
down by P/O. F. Oliver and P/O. J.H. Pickering
in Spitfires from No. 66 Squadron during an
armed reconnaissance over the Channel. Crashed
into the sea off Gurnard's Head, W of St. Ives,
Cornwall.

28 May 1941   He111 P-4   6./KG55
Gl+KP   Wk Nr 2978   (P) Ltn. Eitel Barth,
(O) Uffz. Lenhardt (W) Fw. Wiedemann, (FE) Fw.
Martin Wallrabenstein and (G) Uffz. Mandl.
Ditched in the Channel after being attacked and
damaged by fighters. The crew were rescued safely
by the 3-Seenothalbflottille L'Aberwrach.

*While I, II, and III Gruppen of KG55 were
committed to operations on the Russian Front,
IV./KG55 remained in the west until May 1944.
During that time the unit took part in a small
number of missions against Britain in addition to
their training role.*

8/9 March 1942   He111 H-2   10./KG55
Gl+KU   Wk. Nr. 5393   (P) Ofw. Engelbert
Beisser (67016/119), (O) Oblt. Anton Schneider
(67016/60), (W) Fw. Willi Walz (67016/74) and
(FE.) Fw. Gustav Kuberka (51558/119) all
missing. Failed to return from a mission to Hull,
Yorkshire. Reported to have crashed into the River
Humber, Yorkshire.

27 July 1942   He111 H-3   Stab IV./
KG55   Gl+EW, Wk. Nr. 6858   Ofw (W) Heinz
Zander (67017/30) was slightly wounded by night
fighter. Returned to Dijon/Longvic aerodrome,
France, after being attacked over Swansea, South
Wales.

31 July 1942   He111 H-6   Stab IV./
KG55   Gl+GV   Wk. Nr. 7526   (P) Ofw.
Richard Bock (67017/31) PoW, (O) Hpt.
Adalbert Karbe (67017/3) killed (W) Ofw.
Wilhelm Becker (58246/307) PoW, (FE) Fw.
Hans Delatron (67019/179) killed, (G) Ogfr.
Erhard Schäffer (67019/126) killed. Shot down by
P/O B.R. Keele and P/O G.H. Cowles in a
Beaufighter from No. 604 Squadron during a
mission to Birmingham. Crashed at Coombe
Valley, NW of Preston, Dorset.

12 December 1942   He111 12./KG 55.
(P) Uffz. Friedrich Friedmann (58280/238), (W)
Uffz. Willi Hartnagel, (FE) Gfr. Edgar Koschel
(58280/207), (G) Ogfr. Fritz Krause (58280/
164), (G) Ogfr. Georg Rockel (58280/224) all
killed. Crashed during a training flight, the
cause was not known. Crashed Nr Chalone-sur-
Saone, SW of Dijon, France.

1 February 1943   He111 10/KG 55.
(P) Ofw. Heinrich Lüssmann and (FE) Ofw. Kurt
Rockmann (71042/83) killed. Crashed Nr.
Gevrey-Chambertin, SW of Dijon, France.

14 May 1943   He111 IV/KG 55
Wk.Nr. 3222   Crashed Nr Dijon, France,
probably during a training flight. Ltn. Karl-Heinz
Zehnter killed.

21 May 1943   He111 12./KG55
Gl+KW   Wk. Nr. 4709   (P) Ofw. Rudolf
Dantert, (P) Ofw. Rolf Lindner (53616/143), (O)
Uffz. Reinhold Keinath (58280/293), (W) Ofw.
Helmut Pilch (4.Üb.Staffel Tilsit) and (FE) Ogfr.
Julius Fangmann all killed. Shot down during a
night training flight by F/O Crome in a Mosquito
from No. 29 Squadron. Crashed Nr. Longecourt,
12 km E of Dijon, France.

5 June 1943   He111 IV/KG 55
Wk. Nr. 7778   Uffz Erich Krause (53616/146)
killed. Crashed, probably during a training flight, 7
km. SE of Dijon/Longvic aerodrome, France.

19 June 1943   He111 11./KG 55
Gl+QV (P) Ltn. Josef Hödl (67452/243), (O) Gfr. Siegfried Rohr (674521/318), (W) Uffz. Ferdinand Merschmann and (FE) Ogfr. Frank Schönlebe (67452/299) all killed. Crashed during a training flight Nr. Niederbronn, NW of Haguenau, France.

24 August 1943   He111 10./KG55
Gl+HU (P) Ltn. Götz Graefe, injured, (O) Fw. Erich Schulz, injured, (W) Fw. Wilhelm Pfeifer injured, (W) Uffz. Friedrich Drommard, killed, (FE) Ofw. Willi Laue injured and (G) Gfr. Werner Kirchner, injured. Force landed during a formation training flight at St.-Jean-de-Loone, SE of Dijon, France.

29 September 1943 He111 12./KG55
Gl+BV Crashed on landing on Dijon/Longvic aerodrome, France, following a training flight. (P) Uffz. Wilhelm Petry, injured, (O) Uffz. Kurt Küster injured, (W) Fw Heinz Beu injured and (FE) Ogfr. Kurt Wittenbecher (67452/315) killed.

15 October 1943   He111 10./KG55
Gl+OM (P) Gfr. Emil Benz (A.F.A.R.43 Nr. 1668), (O) Uffz. Franz Huber (53578/565), (O) Uffz. Heinz Pirwitz (67185/360), (W) Gfr. Friedrich Niebrügge and (FE) Ogfr. Ernst Albert (67185/341) all killed. Crashed during a training flight W. of Sennecey-les-Dijon, France.

28 October 1943   He111 12./KG55
Gl+MW (P) Fw. Fritz Müller, (W) Gfr. Alfred Schmidt and (FE) Gfr. Fritz Weller injured. Belly landed due to an engine fire Nr Annoire, Jura Mountains, French/Swiss border.

12 November 1943 He 111 10./KG 55
Gl+NM Wk. Nr. 4795 (P) Uffz. Günter Szlackat (53617/130), (O) Gfr. Hans Biegler-König (552543 I./F.A.R.), (W) Gfr. Helmut Gruner (67185/402), (FE) Uffz. Fritz Ebert (F.A.R. 13 Nr.3664) and (G) Gfr. Rudolf Seiffert (4./F.A.R.53 Nr. 3341), all killed. Crashed during a training flight, Nr Etevaux, E of Dijon. The cause is not recorded.

23 November 1943 He 111 12./KG 55
Gl+NW (P) Uffz. Friedrich Mehr (58280/401), (O) Uffz. Franz Grosser (58286/428), (W) Uffz. Anton Frank (58280/399) and (FE) Fw. Werner Flemming (58280/374), all killed. Crashed during a training flight, Nr Les Mailles. Cause is not recorded.

26 November 1943 He111 10./KG55
Gl+CM Wk. Nr. 7882 (P) Ofw. Heinrich Euler (62873/21), (O) Ogfr. Martin Weiss (Jgd.Fl.Sch. Schleissheim Nr. 546), (W) Uffz. Irimbert Engelbrecht (Ln.E.Kp.19/Lg 3 Nr 883) and (1.Wart) Fw. Josef Gatzmanga (67015/96) all killed. Crashed probably during a training flight, at Melun St. Assise, SE of Paris, France.

14 December 1943 He111 10./KG 55
Gl + IM (P) Ofw. Friedrich Mohrhardt (53578/525), (P) Uffz. Helmut Stirle (67185/395), (O) Uffz. Franz Weinekötter (67185/405), (W) Ogfr. Wolfgang Leitzgen (Ln.Fu.Brs.Kp.m18 Nr 512) and (FE) Uffz. Albert Schönecker (71034/134) all killed. Crashed during a navigational exercise at Poleymieux, Nr. Lyon, France.

16 December 1943 He111 10./KG55
Gl+DM (P) Uffz. Wilhelm Hoche (2./A.Fl.Ausb.31 Nr 1672), (O) Ogfr. Willi Schellenberger (F.A.R.62 Nr 1391), (W) Uffz. Josef Heinz (sch.F.A.R.33 Nr 168) and (FE) Flgr. Benedikt Marschewski (schw.Flak.B.A.11 Nr 1419) all killed. Crashed Nr Crimolois, E of Dijon/Longvic aerodrome, after collision with G1+GM.

16 December 1943 He111 10./KG 55
G1+GM (P) FJOfw. Georg Stein (67021/164), (P) Uffz. Josef Meding (4.Res.12 Nr. 157), (O) Gfr. Herbert Reis (12.Flak. Rgt. Nr.1277), (W) Uffz. Erich Gürtler (Ln.Kp.Fl.Br. Nr. 932) and (FE) Ogfr. Kurt Krause (4.F.A.R.11 Schönwalde Nr.1049) all killed. Crashed Nr Crimolois after collision with G1+DM.

22 January 1944 He111 11./KG55
Gl+EV (P) Uffz. Friedrich Lüdecke (67452/433), (O) Uffz. Paul Stolte (65124/269), (W) Uffz. Josef Hofer (67452/396) and (G) Gfr. Theodor Strohmeyer (67452/437) all killed. Crashed whilst flying on one engine Nr. St. Aubin, S of Orleans, France.

26 January 1944 He111 12./KG55
Gl+OM (P) Uffz. Josef Geis, (O) Uffz. Helmut Ehreiser, (W) Uffz. Walter Hilbrich and (G) Uffz. Erich Bähren (58280/418) all killed. Forced to land due to an engine fire at Münchhausen, SW of Kassel, Germany.

5 February 1944 He111 11./KG 55
Gl+RV (P) Uffz. Otto Dress (67452/469), (O) Ogfr. Ernst Albert (67452/462), (W) Gfr. Hartmut Gehler (67452/473) and (FE) Ofw. Karl Haselbeck (58246/432) all killed. Crashed after being attacked by an intruder during a training flight and crashed Nr. Bourges, SE of Orleans, France.

23 April 1944 He111 P-4 13./KG55
G1+CX Wk. Nr. 2979 (O) Uffz. Franz Richter (17.ELN.17 Nr 620), seriously wounded. Shot down by Mustangs from No. 122 Squadron and crashed at Saulon-la-Chapelle, 12 km SE of Dijon, France.

23 April 1944 He111 H-15 12./KG55 Gl+MW Wk. Nr. 8255 (P) Ofhr. Max Schmidtberger (58280/557) killed, (P) Fw. Walter Fock (58280/252) killed, (W) Uffz. Jakob Deckers (58280/158) killed, (W) Uffz. Walter Hecke (67412/156) seriously wounded, and (G) Uffz. Helmut Michalczik (58280/419) killed. Shot down by Mustangs from No. 122 Squadron and crashed E of Villy-le-Brûlé, SW of Dijon, France.

23 April 1944 He111 H-6 12./KG55
Gl+QW Wk. Nr. 7573 (O) Ofw. Heinz Pries (73045/246) killed. Crashed after attack by Mustangs from No. 122 Squadron at Rouvres, SE of Dijon, France.

23 April 1944 He111 10./KG55
G1+MU Wk. Nr.161387 (P) Uffz. Hans Langbehn, (O) Hpt. Oskar Dettke, (O Trainee) Gfr. Sarganek, (W) Uffz. Kurt Dege (18.Ln.Rgt.12 Nr 1106) wounded and (FE) Ogfr. Hans Schmitt (2.F.A.R. 52 Nr 1833) killed. Force landed after being attacked by Mustangs from No. 122 Squadron on Dijon/Longvic aerodrome, France.

23 April 1944 He111 11./KG55
Gl+SV (P) Uffz. Waldemar Weers, (O) Ogfr. Horst Haase, (W) Gfr. Günther Wieland and (FE) Gfr. Theodor Teckentrup all injured. Landed at Dijon/Longvic aerodrome after attack by Mustangs from No. 122 Squadron.

4 May 1944 He111 H-6 12./KG55
Gl+IW Wk. Nr. 7629 (P) Ofw. Hardy Kowalke (53576/947) wounded, (O) Uffz. Heinz Burzlaff (58280/379) killed, and (FE) Ofw. Wilhelm Eggers (58280/572) wounded. Shot down during a training flight by W/Cdr. G. H. Goodman DFC and F/O. W. F. E. Thomas in a Mosquito of No. 151 Squadron on a Ranger Sortie.

4 May 1944 He111 H-6 12./KG55
G1+NW Wk. Nr. 7215 (W) Gfr. Karl-Heinz Möller (58280/584) wounded and (G) Gfr. Walter Drescher (58280/585) wounded. Shot down during a training flight by W/Cdr. G. H. Goodman DFC and F/O. W. F. E. Thomas in a Mosquito of No. 151 Squadron on a Ranger Sortie.

4 May 1944 He111 H-6 13./KG55
Gl+EX Wk. Nr. 7974 (P) Ogfr. Helmut Kleinmichel (5./F.A.R.26 Nr 89), (W) Gfr. Heinz Jürgens (270 - Ln.Fu.Brs.Kp.2 Nr 303), (FE) Ogfr. Ewald Klein (F.A.R.43 Nr 2852) and (FE) Gfr. Brich Amberg (58280/559) all killed. Shot down during a training flight by W/Cdr. G. H. Goodman DFC and F/O. W. F. E. Thomas in a Mosquito of No. 151 Squadron on a Ranger Sortie. Crashed S of Ouges, SW of Dijon/Longvic aerodrome.

12 September 1944 He111 13./KG55
Gl+MX (O) Ltn. Willi Schnitger (67452/303) killed and Uffz. Gustav Heckmann wounded. Hit by A.A. fire over Royan, S of La Rochelle, France during an operational mission.

5 October 1944 He111 9./KG55
(Transportgruppe 30) S3+IK (P) Fw. Gerhard Meyer (58280/388) killed, (O) Uffz. Engelbert Haser (58280/430) killed, (W) Uffz. Johann Fisch injured, (FE) Fw. Franz Grabmeier injured and (G) Uffz. Rudolf Gebhardt (58280/356) killed. Crashed during an operational mission on Zellhausen aerodrome, S of Frankfurt, Germany.

6 October 1944 He111 9./KG55
(Transportgruppe 30) S3+KK (O) Ltn. Wolfgang Glieden, wounded. Shot down by A.A. fire during an operational mission and crashed Nr Saarburg, SW of Trier, Germany.

14 October 1944 He111 9./KG55
(Transportgruppe 30) S3+AK (P) Oblt. Dieter Ludewig (69876/62) killed and (O) Uffz. Josef Weber injured. Crashed during an operational mission at Grossostheim, SW of Aschaffenburg, Germany.

15 October 1944   He111 8./KG55
Al+BN (Sic. KG53)   (P) Fw. Heinz
Kirchmeyer (58280/460), (O) Fw. Karl Krupitza
(69044/71), (W) Uffz. Josef Schillings (67185/
166), (FE) Ogfr. Fritz Schollmeyer and (G) Uffz.
Hugo Friedrich (214353/89) all killed. Crashed
during a non-operational flight on Giessen
aerodrome, N of Frankfurt, Germany.

31 October 1944   He111 8./KG55
(Transportgruppe 30) S3+LS   (P) Fw. Walter
Merz, (O) Uffz. Josef Huemer, (W) Uffz. Ludwig
Endres, (FE) Ogfr. Heinrich Dziuba and (G) Uffz.
Bruno Speer all missing. Crashed into the sea off
Royan. S of La Rochelle, France, during an
operational mission.

2 November 1944   He111 7./KG55
(Transportgruppe 30) S3+DR   (P) Uffz.
Wilhelm Ganz, (O) Uffz. Karl Reissmann, (W)
Ogfr. Walter König, (FE) Gfr. Friedrich Wenzel
and (G) Gfr. Dietrich Zander all missing. Crashed
into the sea off Dunkirk, France, after being hit by
A.A. fire.

6 November 1944   He111 7./KG55
(Transportgruppe 30) S3+DR   (P) Fw.
Theodor Haller killed, (O) Fw. Wilhelm
Hettlinger killed, (W) Fw. Heinz Rackel killed,
(FE) Ogfr. Walter Albert died of injuries and (G)
Uffz. Ewald Franz injured. Crashed on a non-
operational flight into a mountain called
Hornisgrinde, W of Besenfeld, S of Baden-Baden,
Germany.

7 November 1944   He111 8./KG55
(Transportgruppe 30) S3+HS   (P) Uffz. Rolf
Hackemesser killed. (O) Ogfr. Friedrich Sasse
killed, (W) Ogfr. Karl-Heinz Möller (58280/584)
killed, (FE) Ogfr. Gerhard Ehrich injured and (G)
Uffz. Otto Benecke injured. Crashed during a non-
operational flight at Reifenberg, Taunus, NW of
Frankfurt, Germany.

12 December 1944   Bf109 6./KG(J)55
BT+KB (P) Fw. Heinrich Schiffgen (67185/452)
killed. Crashed during a training flight Nr.
Plattling, Niederbayern, SE of Regensburg.
Germany.

20 December 1944   Bf109 4./KG(J)55
(P) Oblt. J. Dieter Berking. injured. Involved in a
taxying accident on Plattling aerodrome, SE of
Regensburg, Germany.

23 December 1944   FW190 8./KG(J)55
DX+NU (P) Ofhr.z.See Lothar Kleinert (58246/
713) killed. Crashed on take off for a training
flight, on Landau aerodrome, SW of Plattling,
Germany.

1 January 1945   Bf109 G-14
2./KG(J)55. (P) Ofhr. Siegfried Köhler, was
injured. Crashed during a training flight Nr.
Straubing, SE of Regensburg, Germany.

4 January 1945   Bf109 5./KG(J)55
BT+EZ (P) Oblt. Alfred Veith, seriously injured.
Collided with PZ+TX during a training flight Nr
Plattling, SE of Regensburg, Germany.

4 January 1945   Bf109 5./KG(J)55
PZ+TX (P) Uffz. Brich Barein (58280/414),
killed. Collided with BT+EZ during a training
flight Nr Plattling.

4 January 1945   Arado Ar 96 9./KG55
Wk. Nr. 550805 (P) Uffz. Fridolin Wenzel
injured. Rammed during a formation training
flight and crashed Nr Haidlfing, NE of Landau, SE
of Regensburg, Germany.

10 January 1945   Bf109 1./KG(J)55
Wk. Nr. 413766 (P) Fw. Arthur Böttger (68578/
763) killed. Crashed during a training flight Nr
Haimbuch/Regensburg, Germany.

10 January 1945   Bf 109 5./KG(J)55
DX+KG   (P) Ofw. Wilhelm Stelzner
(67020/137) killed. Crashed during a training
flight on Plattling aerodrome, SE of Regensburg,
Germany.

12 February 1945   Bf109 G-6
1./KG(J)55. (P) Hpt. Wolfgang Witte (67013/
118) Staffelkapitän, seriously injured. He died of
his injuries on the 22. 2.1945. Crashed during a
training flight Nr Leiblfing, SW of Straubing,
Germany.

16 February 1945   Bf109 5./KG(J)55
Wk. Nr. 165836 (P) Ofw. Horst Schaufuss
(67185/359) killed. Crashed during a training
flight on Plattling aerodrome, Germany.